SOMI
ANUNTRA MILLER
————— & —————
PATRICIA LAKE

THAI
COOKING
✸ CLASS ✸

PHOTOGRAPHY ASHLEY BARBER
STYLING MICHELLE GORRY

BAY BOOKS

SYDNEY AND LONDON

CONTENTS

Editor: Ingaret Ward
Designer: Ivy Hansen

© text Patricia Lake
and Somi Anuntra Miller

Published by Bay Books
61–69 Anzac Parade
Kensington NSW 2033

National Library of Australia
card number and ISBN 1 86256 073 0

BB88

Printed by Toppan Printing Co. in Singapore
Typeset by Savage Type Pty Ltd, Brisbane,
Queensland

ACKNOWLEDGEMENTS
The publisher would like to thank the following
for their assistance during the production of
this book:
Abigail Walsh for her help to Michelle Gorry;
Accoutrement, Mosman; Appley Hoare
Antiques, Mosman; Country Form Furniture,
Double Bay; Dansab Pty Ltd, Chippendale;
Gallery Nomad, Paddington; Good Luck
Grocery Store Pty Ltd, Sydney; Lifestyle
Imports, Chippendale; Made in Japan Imports
NSW, Neutral Bay; Made Where, Double Bay;
Mid City House and Garden, Sydney.

THAI CUISINE

Welcome to one of the world's great cuisines. This is food you can enjoy cooking as much as eating. Wonderful tastes can be created in your own kitchen with utensils you already have and a minimum of fuss.

Most of the recipes in this book are simple and take less than half an hour to cook. They are traditional recipes, prepared with Western cooks in mind. We tell you where to find the ingredients easily, how to prepare and cook the food correctly and how to use substitutes

Thai food combines the best of several Eastern cuisines: the oriental bite of Szechuan Chinese, the tropical flavour of Malaysian, the creamy coconut sauces of Southern Indian and the aromatic spices of Arabian food.

Thais then add an abundance of fresh ingredients , coriander plants, chillies and pepper. The result is like a 'cuisine minceur' of the Orient. Small portions of lean meat, poultry and seafood, and plenty of fresh vegetables and salads.

Thai food is lightly cooked so it's crisp, colourful, sharply flavoured and nutritious. The distinctive taste comes from a handful of fundamental ingredients, all of them widely available at Asian foodstores and delicatessens:

- fresh coriander, including the roots
- fresh basil, mint and lemon grass
- garlic, chillies, pepper, onion and shallots
- coconut milk
- shrimp paste and fish sauce
- citrus leaves, especially Kaffir lime leaves
- and occasionally dried spices.

Like the word 'Thai' (which means free), Thai cooks are never rigid in their approach. So be flexible in your interpretation of the recipes, particularly if you're not always able to find every ingredient. If you embrace their style and imagination, you'll find your venture into Thai cooking an extremely pleasurable and rewarding one.

It can be economical, too, if you adapt recipes to take advantage of market and seasonal bargains. For instance, Green Sweet Chicken Curry is equally delicious if you use beef, fish or pork instead of chicken.

Good results come with careful planning, quick, vigilant cooking and imaginative presentation. Above all, taste as you cook. Thai is very tasty food and Thai cooks try to strike a balance between sweet, sour, hot, bitter and salty. The cook is meant to enjoy the meal, too. Don't hide in the kitchen preparing course after course. Do what the Thais do and put everything on the table at once and get everyone to help themselves.

Save your stir-fried dishes until last and make soups and curries beforehand. Pre-cooked snacks and rice can be heated at the last minute. As long as the rice is steaming, it doesn't matter if the other dishes aren't particularly hot.

Eat with forks and tablespoons (fork in the left hand to push food on to the spoon in the right hand) as they do in Thailand. The Thais do not scoop portions onto their plates as Westerners tend to do (even when eating at Thai restaurants). Instead, they share from common dishes, taking only enough for a bite or two at a time. This way, one avoids seeming too greedy and everyone has an ample share of each dish. Also, it is easier to savour the tastes of a variety of dishes. An important consequence of this eating pattern is that all food must be 'bite-sized'. Thus, proper cutting of ingredients before cooking is an essential part of Thai cuisine.

THE THAI KITCHEN

A walk through a Thai village is like walking through a huge open-air kitchen. Everywhere you look people seem to be preparing a meal. Everything and everyone is on display.

Few houses have built-in or enclosed kitchens. Cooking takes place under a verandah or in a roughly built annexe with mud floors. If there are any walls at all, the windows are wide and unglazed so the smoke and food aromas can waft away.

The stove is a crude charcoal burner, built of either metal or clay, on which sits a wok or large pot. Because there are no ovens you'll find few baked dishes in Thai cuisine. A wooden cupboard is used to store garlic, fish sauce, dried chillies and dried fish. Large earthenware tubs store

Thai floating market.

rainwater, with lids to keep the dust out.

The Thai kitchen may lack gadgets and shiny surfaces, but it is no place of drudgery. Groups of people sit around slicing and chopping, snacking and laughing. The village news and gossip is digested as the next meal is being prepared, and a visitor's offer of help will be rewarded with an invitation to stay for dinner.

Apart from several woks, saucepans and steamers, the most important items in a Thai kitchen are sharp knives and cleavers, some chopping boards, a coconut shredder and a mortar and pestle.

If the Thais are able to improvise with so few utensils, so can we. A wok is a worthwhile investment, but a deep-frying pan will do. A large multi-layered bamboo steamer would be handy, but a cheap fold-out metal one is just as effective, and while it feels good to grind away your frustrations with a mortar and pestle, a food processor, grinder or blender will save a lot of time. If you decide to buy a mortar and pestle, buy one from Thailand. Because the mortar is ceramic and the pestle wood, they're specially designed to cope with moist curry pastes and for bruising lemon grass, citrus rind, garlic and coriander roots. Best of all, they're the cheapest. A Thai mortar and pestle sells for about the same price as the average wok — the cost of one or two main course dishes at your local Thai restaurant!

While village life in Thailand allows time for daily marketing and traditional making of pastes, stocks and sauces, the urban and middle income Thai families face many of the time restraints we do.

So there is no dishonour in using a food processor instead of a mortar and pestle or any form of shortcut, for that matter, if the end result tastes good. Thai cooks use many shortcuts to make life easier. Ready-made curry pastes, chilli sauces, powdered soup stocks and dried ingredients are commonplace in Bangkok's supermarkets and are widely available in Asian foodstores outside Thailand.

You'll find many ingredients can be frozen and then thawed successfully in a microwave oven. Homemade curry pastes and sauces are worth the effort, but make large quantities and freeze them in measured amounts. Even the roots and stems of coriander and lemon grass can be frozen in plastic wrap. A variety of soup stocks and small individual portions of chicken, beef and pork will always come in handy for quick defrosting in the microwave.

It is important, however, to use fresh herbs, vegetables and seafood wherever possible, and to plan your menus around the best seasonal produce available.

Most stores specialising in Asian groceries outside Asia now have comprehensive Thai sections and basics like canned coconut milk, fish sauce, noodles and dried chillies and spices are cheaper at supermarkets. Some delicatessens and health food stores even stock ingredients like tamarind pulp, powdered galangal and dried lemon grass. If you do have local Asian grocers, get to know them, tell them you're interested in Thai cooking and ask for advice on ingredients. With demand on the increase, more Thai items are becoming available.

If you don't have a local Asian foodstore, one visit to your nearest city's Chinatown will do — once you have a stock of fundamentals, they'll last a long time.

A word about the cooking routine: always read a recipe from beginning to end before you start. Assemble all the ingredients around you, then prepare. Advice on cutting methods can be found on pages 46–49. Make sure you have your pre-cut ingredients and pre-measured condiments and spices for each dish handy to the stove. A good idea is to place them in separate little piles on a large plate, one plate for each recipe. That way you don't get confused if you're cooking several items at once. It's a useful habit to get into and one Thai cooks use.

Many varieties of chilli are available.

MEASURING EQUIPMENT

In this book, fresh ingredients such as fish or meat, are given in grams so you know how much to buy. A small, inexpensive set of kitchen scales is always handy and very easy to use.

Other ingredients in our recipes are given in tablespoons and cups, so you will need a nest of measuring cups (1 cup, ½ cup, ⅓ cup and ¼ cup); a set of spoons (1 tablespoon, 1 teaspoon, ½ teaspoon and ¼ teaspoon); and a transparent graduated measuring jug (1 litre or 250 mL) for measuring liquids. Cup and spoon measures are always level.

Standard metric measures:

4 cups	1 litre (32 fl. oz., 2 pints U.S.A.)
1 cup	250 mL (8 fl. oz., ½ pint U.S.A.)
1 tablespoon	20 mL
1 teaspoon	5 mL

STARTERS AND SNACKS

It's not customary in Thailand to have starters or an entree at meal times, but the Thai people are inveterate snackers. At parties or celebrations much of the food served is snack food with wonderful sauces.

Credit: Lifestyle Imports; Made in Japan Imports; Country Farm

SPICY DEEP-FRIED FISH CAKES
(TOD MAN PLA)

1 kg redfish fillets (or similar type fish)
4 tablespoons red curry paste, bought or homemade (see recipe)
100 g green beans, finely sliced into 3 mm pieces
1 tablespoon dried lime leaves (soaked 10 minutes, then sliced)
2 tablespoons finely chopped fresh coriander leaves and root
1 egg, lightly beaten
2 teaspoons sugar
½ teaspoon salt
about 1½ cups (400 mL) vegetable oil, for deep-frying

TO SERVE
fresh coriander sprigs
sliced cucumber
sliced tomato
Sweet and Sour Cucumber Relish (see recipe)

Steam fish, then flake with a fork. Put fish and curry paste into a food processor and blend to a light, finely textured consistency. Combine in a bowl with beans, lime leaves, coriander, beaten egg, sugar and salt and knead with your hands until the mixture clings together well. (If it's a little too wet, place uncovered in the refrigerator for 30 minutes to chill and dry a little.)

Roll into balls then shape into 4 cm patties. Deep-fry in a small saucepan or wok, one or two at a time, turning them over if necessary to achieve an all-over golden brown colour.

Serve on a plate, garnished with coriander sprigs, sliced cucumber and tomato, and a side bowl of Sweet and Sour Cucumber Relish.

Serves 6

PRAWN SATAY
(GOONG SATAY)

16 large green (uncooked) prawns, peeled, deveined, tails intact
1 clove garlic, finely chopped
1 teaspoon ground turmeric
1 coriander root, finely chopped
pinch salt
1 teaspoon sugar
1 tablespoon oil
16 bamboo skewers, pre-soaked in water to avoid charring
Satay Sauce (see recipe), to serve

Place prawns in a bowl and sprinkle them with chopped garlic, turmeric, coriander root, salt, sugar and oil. Gently mix prawns with your hands, so prawns are well covered with the marinade. Leave to stand in the refrigerator for at least 20 minutes.

Thread prawns onto satay skewers using one prawn per skewer. Grill or barbecue over strong heat until pink (about 2 minutes each side). Serve with Satay Sauce.

Serves 4

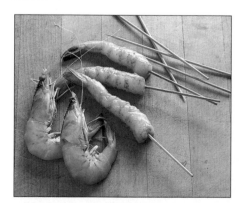

Threading prawns Thai style.

Clockwise from top: Sweet and Sour Cucumber Relish, Spicy Deep-fried Fish Cakes, Prawn Satays, Mixed Satays and Satay Sauce.

MIXED SATAYS

While not strictly Thai, satays are now eaten in Thailand as often as in Indonesia, where they originated. The Thais have simply added lemon grass, shrimp paste (kapi) and coriander roots to the satay sauce to give it a distinctive Thai flavour.

The word 'satay' has been adopted by the Thais too. It's believed the word was originally a corruption of the English word 'steak', though it now applies to the style of cooking meats, or anything, on skewers. Another popular satay in Thailand is toast. It's quite a favourite dipped in satay sauce for a mid-morning snack. Here are some other, more meaty, recipes.

200 g beef,
200 g chicken } cut in 1 cm
200 g pork × 5 cm strips
lettuce leaves, tomato and cucumber slices, to serve
fresh coriander sprigs, to garnish
MARINADE
2 teaspoons ground turmeric
1 tablespoon sugar
pinch salt
1 teaspoon ground coriander
½ teaspoon ground cumin
4 tablespoons vegetable oil
1 tablespoon fish sauce
2 cloves garlic, finely chopped
16 bamboo skewers, pre-soaked in water to avoid charring
TO SERVE
Satay Sauce (see recipe)
Sweet and Sour Cucumber Relish (see recipe)

Thread the meat on to the skewers, 3 or 4 strips to a skewer. Then place in a shallow dish. Combine marinade ingredients in a food processor and blend until smooth. Pour over the satays and marinate for at least an hour, rotating sticks occasionally.

Grill or barbecue over a fierce heat for about 3 minutes each side, turning several times. Place on a bed of lettuce leaves alongside slices of tomato and cucumber. Garnish with fresh coriander. Serve with bowls of Satay Sauce and Sweet and Sour Cucumber Relish.

Serves 4

SWEET AND SOUR CUCUMBER RELISH
(THANG KWA PREOW WAN)

½ cup (125 mL) vinegar
1 cup (250 g) sugar
1 teaspoon salt
3 tablespoons water
1 small onion, finely diced
1 small carrot, finely chopped
1 medium-sized green cucumber, finely chopped
fresh coriander leaves, chopped

Boil vinegar, sugar, salt and water in a saucepan for 1 minute. Mix onion, carrot and cucumber pieces in a serving bowl and pour the syrup over until vegetables are just covered.

Taste to see if extra vinegar, sugar or salt is needed to balance flavours. For those who prefer a spicy cucumber relish, add a finely sliced chilli or some chilli paste. Garnish with chopped coriander leaves and serve with satays, fish cakes and crispy deep-fried snacks.

Makes about 1½ cups (350 mL)

SATAY SAUCE
(NAM JIM SATAY)

1 small onion, chopped
1 tablespoon lemon grass, finely chopped
½ teaspoon shrimp paste
3 dried red chillies or 1 teaspoon chilli powder
2 cloves garlic
½ teaspoon ground cumin
½ teaspoon ground coriander
2 coriander roots, chopped
1 cup (250 mL) coconut milk
1 teaspoon vegetable oil
150 g ground roasted peanuts or crunchy peanut butter
2 tablespoons sugar
2 teaspoons tamarind juice
salt

In a blender, combine the first eight ingredients with enough coconut milk to moisten.

Heat oil in a saucepan and gently stir-fry satay mixture until it turns a pale pinky brown. Add remaining coconut milk, stirring briskly, then reduce heat to low.

Add peanuts and stir well to separate. Then add sugar and tamarind juice and a pinch of salt. If the sauce is too thick, add extra coconut milk. If it's too thin, simmer very gently to reduce — coconut milk and peanuts burn easily.

Serves 4

1. Cut puff pastry sheet into 4 equal pieces.

2. Take 1 piece, corner towards you, place 1 tablespoon mix in centre.

3. Fold, pinching to form a curly border. Put a twist in each wing of pastry.

THAI CURRY PUFFS
(GURI PAK)

700 g prepared puff pastry, slightly thawed
about 1½ cups (400 mL) vegetable oil, for deep-frying

FILLING
1 clove garlic, chopped
4 tablespoons vegetable oil
3 tablespoons sliced onion
1 tablespoon chopped coriander root
1 tablespoon turmeric
300 g lean pork, chicken or beef, minced
1 tablespoon sugar
2 teaspoons salt
1 teaspoon pepper, white or black
200 g cooked mashed potato
2 tablespoons chopped shallots

TO SERVE
Sweet and Sour Cucumber Relish (see recipe)
Satay Sauce (see recipe)

In a wok or frypan, stir-fry garlic until golden in the 4 tablespoons vegetable oil. Add onion, coriander root and turmeric, stir-fry several minutes, then add minced meat, sugar, salt and pepper, and stir-fry until meat is cooked and tender.

Turn down the heat, add potato and stir-fry to mix ingredients well. Taste to see if extra sugar or pepper is needed. Add shallots, stir briefly, then remove from heat. Place in a large bowl to cool.

Take one sheet of puff pastry and cut into four equal pieces. Take one of these small pieces and lay it flat with a corner towards you. Place about 1 tablespoon (more or less according to preference) of the filling in the middle of the square and lift the bottom corner (the one nearest to you) over to meet its opposite corner, forming a triangular parcel. Seal the edges with your fingers, pinching in the pastry to form a curly border, or use a fork to indent a fancy edge. (See *Note*)

Put a twist in each 'wing' of the pastry, towards the centre then away again, place on greaseproof paper and set aside. Repeat until all the mixture is used.

Deep-fry in vegetable oil in a saucepan or wok, frying several at a time until golden brown. Serve with Sweet and Sour Cucumber Relish and Satay Sauce.

Makes about 20

Note: If you prefer, cut out 10 cm-diameter rounds of pastry and brush the edges with water. Place one tablespoon of filling on one side. Fold over and pinch edges together to form 'half moon' curry puffs.

Thai Curry Puffs with Sweet and Sour Cucumber Relish and Satay Sauce.

PRAWN AND PORK TOAST
(KANOM PANG MUU GOONG)

**2 tablespoons finely chopped fresh
  coriander leaves and roots
2 cloves garlic, finely chopped
300 g prawns, finely chopped
250 g minced pork
2 onions, finely chopped
3 tablespoons finely chopped green
  shallot stems
1 egg, lightly beaten
1 teaspoon white pepper
1 tablespoon fish sauce
10 slices stale bread, crusts trimmed
about 1½ cups (400 mL) vegetable oil
  for deep-frying
fresh coriander sprigs, to garnish**

Pound coriander root and garlic together
to make a paste then add to a mixing bowl
with prawns, minced pork, onions, shallots, beaten egg, pepper and fish sauce.
Knead mixture thoroughly with your
hands until it clings together well.

·Spread evenly to a thickness of 1 cm
over bread, making sure it covers the
edges. Cut into the shapes of your
choice, e.g. squares or triangles or use
fancy pastry cutters if you like.

Deep-fry several at a time, meat-side
down first. Fry 1–2 minutes until golden
then turn over and fry the other side.
When golden all over, remove and drain
on absorbent kitchen paper. Keep warm
in the oven until ready to serve. Garnish
with coriander sprigs and serve with dipping sauces of your choice.

Serves 4

SWEET CHILLI DIPPING SAUCE
(NAM JIM WAN)

**100 g pickled plums (see *Note*)
4 large fresh red chillies
3 cloves garlic
½ cup (125 g) sugar
1 teaspoon salt
½ cup (125 mL) vinegar
1 teaspoon tamarind juice (optional)
3 tablespoons water
chopped fresh coriander leaves, to
  garnish**

Boil pickled plums for several minutes in
water. Drain then blend with a little plum
juice for a few seconds in a food
processor. Pour into a saucepan and set
aside.

Roughly blend chillies and garlic then
add to plum puree with the sugar, salt and
vinegar and tamarind juice if using. Simmer mixture for about 10 minutes, taking
care not to let it burn or stick to the bottom of the saucepan. Taste to see if extra
sugar, salt or vinegar is needed. The
flavour should be slightly more sweet
than sour or salty.

Add water to the sauce while cooking,
to maintain the consistency you require.
Garnish with chopped coriander leaves
and serve with Thai snacks, particularly
crisp-fried food. This sauce will keep in
sterilised jars for several weeks in the
refrigerator.

Makes 2–3 cups (500–750 mL)

Note: Available in jars in Asian stores,
sometimes called 'salted' plums.

*Prawn and Pork Toast. Make them any
shape you like, but keep their size
uniform so they cook evenly.*

1. Take 1 bean curd sheet and spoon out half mix in sausage shaped mound down longest edge.

2. Roll up, sealing edge with water and pinching both ends.

3. Steam for 20 minutes.

SAVOURY SEAFOOD ROLLS
(HAE GUEN)

2 sheets beancurd skin (see *Note*)
200 g redfish fillets (or similar fish), bones removed and flesh chopped
200 g raw or cooked prawns
100 g pork fat, chopped
1 small onion, chopped
6 cloves garlic, chopped
3 tablespoons chopped fresh coriander root
1 tablespoon fish sauce
2 teaspoons sugar
2 teaspoons white pepper

TO SERVE
Sliced cucumber and fresh coriander sprigs
Sweet Chilli Dipping Sauce (see recipe)
Sweet and Sour Cucumber Relish (see recipe)

Soak beancurd skins in warm water to soften, then drain. Mix all ingredients except beancurd skin in a bowl and marinate for at least 10 minutes. Process in small batches in a food processor to achieve a fine, lightly textured mixture.

Take one beancurd sheet and spoon out half the mixture in a long sausage-shaped mound down the longest edge.

Roll up, sealing edge with water and pinching both ends. Repeat with remaining half of mixture on the other sheet.

Steam for 20 minutes or deep-fry in a large wok for 1–2 minutes until golden. Drain on absorbent kitchen paper and leave for at least 45 minutes to cool and set firmly.

Slice diagonally into 2 cm thick slices. Allowing 4–6 slices a person, serve as an entree or appetiser to a Thai feast.

Garnish with cucumber and coriander sprigs. Accompany with separate bowls of Sweet Chilli Dipping Sauce and Sweet and Sour Cucumber Relish.

Serves 4

Note: Beancurd sheets or skins are sometimes called dried tofu sheets, and are available from Asian foodstores.

4. Slice diagonally and serve garnished. Allow 4–6 slices per person.

CRISPY PARCELS
(KEIO GROB)

1 clove garlic, chopped
1 onion, chopped
1 tablespoon chopped fresh coriander root
60 g minced pork
60 g finely chopped prawns (cooked or raw)
½ teaspoon salt
1 teaspoon pepper
1 tablespoon sugar
2 carrots, grated
2 tablespoons finely chopped shallots
50 wonton wrappers, fresh or thawed
3 tablespoons cooking oil
about 1½ cups (400 mL) vegetable oil for deep-frying

TO SERVE
Sweet Chilli Sauce (see recipe)
Sweet and Sour Cucumber Relish (see recipe)

In a wok over medium heat, stir-fry garlic until golden. Add onion and coriander root, stir-fry several minutes, then add pork and prawns, salt, pepper and sugar. Stir-fry until pork is cooked. Add carrot and shallots and stir several times. Remove from heat and place in a bowl to cool.

Use double sheets of wonton wrappers at a time, if they appear to be too flimsy. Place them in front of you on top of a damp tea towel, as they dry out easily. Arrange with a wonton wrapper corner towards you. Place one teaspoon of the filling in the centre, moisten the edges of the wonton wrapper with water and fold the bottom corner away from you, using the towel to help you (see photo), and over to the opposite corner, forming a triangular parcel. Press the edges together to seal. Twist each wing of the triangle towards the middle. Repeat until all mixture is used.

Deep-fry several at a time, turning over if necessary until golden (about 2 minutes each). Serve with Sweet Chilli Dipping Sauce and Sweet and Sour Cucumber Relish.

Serves 6

THAI SPRING ROLLS
(POH PIA)

20 spring roll wrappers
1½ teaspoons cornflour mixed with 2 tablespoons water
about 1½ cups (400 mL) vegetable oil, for deep-frying
FILLING
500 g lean pork, chopped into 2 cm cubes
100 g cooked prawns, peeled and chopped
1 tablespoon sliced onion
1 clove garlic, finely chopped
1 tablespoon chopped coriander root
3 tablespoons vegetable oil
1 teaspoon pepper
1 teaspoon salt
1½ tablespoons sugar
2 large carrots, grated
1 tablespoon finely chopped shallots

TO SERVE
sliced cucumber
fresh coriander sprigs
Sweet Chilli Dipping Sauce (see recipe)
Sweet and Sour Cucumber Relish (see recipe)

In a saucepan simmer pork with just enough water to cover the meat for about 20 minutes, until pork is cooked but tender. This reduces the pork's fat and moisture content. Drain, place in a food processor and blend to a fine texture.

In a wok, stir-fry minced pork, prawns, onion, garlic and coriander root in 3 tablespoons vegetable oil, until onion is golden and prawns are pink. Add pepper, salt and sugar, stirring until sugar dissolves. Taste to see if extra pepper or sugar is needed.

Add carrot and stir briefly, then remove from heat. Place in a bowl, sprinkle with chopped shallots, then leave to cool.

Now for the packaging! Use a clean damp cloth or towel to keep the spring roll wrappers damp, as they dry out very quickly. Take one wrapper, lay it on the towel with a corner towards you. Wet all the edges with the paste made from cornflour and water. Place a tablespoon of the filling in the nearest corner to you

then, using the towel to help you, roll corner flap away from you over the mixture. Fold in side corners and roll up, using the towel to keep the wrapper smoothly rolled and damp. Seal the edges with more paste. Repeat with remaining wrappers and filling.

Deep-fry spring rolls in vegetable oil, several at a time, turning them over to get an even golden brown colour. Don't overcook as they become soggy inside. Drain on absorbent kitchen paper.

Serve with sliced cucumber and garnish with coriander sprigs. Accompany with Sweet Chilli Dipping Sauce and Sweet and Sour Cucumber Relish.
Makes 20–30

CRISP FRIED CALAMARI
(PLA MEUK TOD)

1 egg, lightly beaten
1 teaspoon sugar
½ teaspoon salt
½ teaspoon pepper
300 g calamari rings, rinsed, drained and dried
100 g dried breadcrumbs
vegetable oil, for deep-frying
TO SERVE
Sweet Chilli Dipping Sauce (see recipe)

Mix egg, sugar, salt and pepper in a bowl and marinate calamari for about 10 minutes.

Remove calamari and drain in a colander for 20 minutes. (Reserve the egg mixture for later use as an omelette if you like.)

Lightly cover calamari with breadcrumbs. Deep-fry in vegetable oil in a wok or saucepan, cooking several at a time, until golden. Serve with Sweet Chilli Dipping Sauce.

Serves 4

Serve Thai Spring Rolls with Sweet Chilli Dipping Sauce and Sweet and Sour Cucumber Relish.

1. *Place wonton wrapper on damp teatowel with corner of wrapper towards you. Place 1 teaspoon filling in centre.*

2. *Use towel to fold over to opposite corner forming a triangular parcel.*

3. *Twist wings and deep fry.*

RICE, NOODLES AND THAI SAUCES

Rice is the mainstay of the Thai diet. Spicy sauces are often served as a condiment and make a delicious dish out of a bowl of rice or noodles.

Plain, unsalted rice is served with main meals. Sticky or glutinous rice is reserved for sweet dishes.

Noodles came to Thailand with the Chinese. Thais like to stir-fry noodles with a variety of meats and vegetables, or make them the basis of a hearty soup!

SWEET AND SOUR CRISP-FRIED THAI NOODLES
(MEE GROB)

220 g (dried weight) rice vermicelli
3 cups (750 mL) vegetable oil
2 eggs, beaten for omelette strips
1 knob pickled garlic, sliced and stir-fried until golden (see *Note*)
100 g lean pork, finely sliced
100 g prawns, peeled
2 tablespoons bottled tomato sauce
2 tablespoons sugar
2 tablespoons lemon juice
1 tablespoon sliced grapefruit peel
1 tablespoon fish sauce
4 tablespoons shallots or garlic chives, sliced into 2.5 cm pieces

GARNISH
fresh coriander leaves
sliced fresh red chilli
shallot curls

Take a plastic shopping bag and break up the noodles inside it, otherwise you'll be finding bits of broken noodles for weeks. Heat oil in a wok until it's very hot, and deep-fry noodles in small batches. It requires vigilant cooking, as the noodles puff up very quickly and must be removed immediately with a slotted spoon and placed on absorbent kitchen paper to drain.

Put noodles aside. Drain off most of the oil and reserve for another time, leaving about 3 tablespoons in the wok.

In another pan, make a very thin omelette from the beaten egg. When cooked, fold over on itself several times, place on a chopping board and cut into fine strips. Put aside.

Take half the pickled garlic and stir-fry it in remaining oil in the wok. Add pork, stir-fry until golden, then add prawns and cook briefly until they turn pink.

Now add the tomato sauce, sugar, lemon juice, grapefruit peel and fish sauce and stir-fry until sugar has dissolved and peel turns golden. Add crisp-fried noodles, toss several times, sprinkle with chopped shallots and turn out onto serving platter. Garnish with omelette strips, coriander leaves, chilli, shallot curls and remaining garlic.

Serves 4

Note: Pickled garlic can be bought in most Asian foodstores, or you can make your own (see recipe).

STIR-FRIED GLASS NOODLES WITH VEGETABLES
(PAD WOON SEN)

150 g (dried weight) cellophane noodles
3 tablespoons vegetable oil
1 clove garlic, finely chopped
1 carrot, thinly sliced
3 tablespoons water or stock
½ small stalk celery, sliced
50 g Chinese cabbage, shredded
1 tablespoon oyster sauce
1 tablespoon fish sauce
1 teaspoon sugar
pinch pepper

Soak the noodles in warm water for 5 minutes, then drain them well. Put aside.

In a wok fry garlic in vegetable oil until golden, then add carrot and stir-fry for 1 minute. Add water and all remaining ingredients, except noodles, stirring gently. Cook 1–2 minutes, then add noodles and toss so that ingredients are well combined and noodles are heated thoroughly.

Serves 4

Stir-fried Glass Noodles with Vegetables and Sweet and Sour Crisp-fried Thai Noodles.

15

SPICY SAUCES

CHILLI FISH SAUCE
(NAM PLA PRIK)

3 large fresh chillies, finely sliced
1 clove garlic, finely sliced or minced
4 tablespoons lemon juice
5 tablespoons fish sauce

Stir all ingredients together in a bowl. Serve in shallow bowls as an accompaniment to traditional Thai meals.

Makes about ½ cup (125 mL)

SOUR FISH SAUCE
(NAM PLA MANAO)

4 tablespoons lemon juice
5 tablespoons fish sauce

Stir ingredients together in a bowl and pour into shallow serving bowls. Serve as an accompaniment to traditional Thai meals, especially as a condiment for noodles and soups.

Makes about ½ cup (125 mL)

CRAB DIP
(POO LON)

Unlike the nam priks, which are uncooked dipping sauces (sometimes with cooked ingredients), lons are boiled dipping sauces. Lons are usually served with fried fish, raw vegetables, rice or noodles.

1½ cups (375 mL) thick coconut milk
200 g crabmeat (fresh or canned), flaked
1 medium-sized onion, finely chopped
¼ teaspoon sugar
salt and pepper
2 teaspoons tamarind or lemon juice
2 fresh chillies, finely sliced or ½ tablespoon roasted chilli paste, bought or homemade (see recipe)
1 tablespoon chopped fresh coriander leaves

In a saucepan bring coconut milk to the boil, add crabmeat and simmer for 5 minutes, stirring occasionally. Add onion, sugar, salt, pepper, tamarind juice and sliced chillies, and simmer until sauce thickens. Taste to see if extra sugar, salt, pepper or tamarind juice is needed. Remove from heat and serve sprinkled with coriander leaves.

Serves 4

FLAKED FISH AND TAMARIND SAUCE
(NAM PRIK THA DANG)

This spicy sauce can make a meal out of a bowl of rice or noodles.

100 g dried red chillies, stalks removed
4 tablespoons vegetable oil, for frying
1 onion, chopped
2 tablespoons chopped garlic
1 tablespoon chopped coriander root
2 teaspoons shrimp paste
1 tablespoon sugar
1 tablespoon lemon juice
1 tablespoon tamarind juice
2 tablespoons fish sauce
200 g white-fleshed fish, flaked

In a wok or frypan, stir-fry chillies over medium heat in half the oil. Remove chillies and set aside. Brown onion, add garlic and coriander root and stir-fry for several minutes. Remove and place beside chillies. Using the rest of the oil, slowly fry shrimp paste, browning each side without burning.

In a food processor, combine all ingredients except flaked fish, with a little boiled water to moisten if necessary. Process until ingredients are well mixed but not mushy.

Pour into a bowl and stir fish flakes into the sauce. Taste to see if extra lemon juice, sugar or fish sauce is needed. The sauce should taste spicy and slightly sweet, sour and salty. It will keep for a day or two refrigerated in a sterilised jar.

Makes 2–3 cups (500–750 mL)

No traditional Thai meal is complete without at least one bowl of a spicy hot sauce, or nam prik. From left, Sour Fish Sauce, Chilli Fish Sauce, Crab Dip, Flaked Fish and Tamarind Sauce, Chilli Vinegar with Garlic and Ginger, Hot and Sour Chilli Sauce, and Spicy Dried Shrimp Sauce.

CHILLI VINEGAR WITH GARLIC AND GINGER
(NAM JIM ROT DED)

This special sauce will keep indefinitely if properly stored. It's an extremely hot chilli dipping sauce for meats, or condiment for noodles and soups. Be very careful when preparing, and wash your hands with lemon juice (after first scrubbing the chilli off them). Store out of reach of children and warn your guests this sauce is fiery. Scale the recipe down if you don't want a large batch.

½ cup (125 mL) water
3 cups (750 mL) vinegar
½ cup (125 mL) fish sauce
3 tablespoons sugar
1 teaspoon salt
1 kg fresh red chillies (preferably small hot ones), stems removed
4 tablespoons peeled, chopped garlic
4 tablespoons sliced fresh ginger root
4 tablespoons chopped whole coriander plant (including root)

In a large saucepan, bring water, vinegar, fish sauce, sugar and salt to the boil. Boil for 30 seconds, then remove from heat. Taste to see if sauce needs extra vinegar, sugar or salt. Stand saucepan in a tray of cold water to cool.

In a food processor, blend chilli, garlic, ginger and coriander until fine. Pour this paste into the cooled vinegar syrup. Add more vinegar if there's not enough liquid to cover the chilli mixture or if you'd like a thinner sauce. The consistency is a matter of choice, either a thick paste or a thinner sauce. Store in sterilised glass jars with tightly fitting lids.

Makes about 1.5 litres

HOT AND SOUR CHILLI SAUCE
(NAM PRIK KEEGA)

This chilli sauce is delicious with barbecued prawns, fish and pork but is also eaten in Thailand with rice and salads. Take great care when preparing the chillies. Always wash your hands after chopping them and never touch your eyes while preparing chillies.

100 g fresh red chillies
100 g fresh green chillies
1 tablespoon vegetable oil
1 onion, chopped
2 tablespoons chopped garlic
1 tablespoon chopped coriander root
1 tablespoon lemon juice
1 tablespoon fish sauce
2 tablespoons chopped fresh coriander leaves
2 tablespoons finely chopped shallots

Remove stalks from chillies, then saute them in a little oil. Remove and set aside. Saute onion, garlic and coriander root, stir-frying for several minutes. Remove from heat. In a food processor, carefully process chillies, onion, garlic and coriander root so that the sauce is not too mushy.

Place mixture in a bowl and stir in lemon juice and fish sauce. If the sauce is too thick, add a little boiled water. Taste to see if extra fish sauce or lemon juice is needed. There should be a balance between hot, sour and salty flavours.

Stir in coriander leaves and shallots just before serving. This sauce will last several weeks in the refrigerator, providing you don't add the coriander or shallots until just before serving.

Makes about 625 mL

SPICY DRIED SHRIMP SAUCE
(NAM PRIK KAPI)

An old-fashioned style of spicy sauce to accompany deep-fried fish, omelettes, soups, vegetables or plain rice. To get the rough consistency of the original you need to use a mortar and pestle and pound by hand.

2 tablespoons shrimp paste
3 cloves garlic, chopped
5 fresh red chillies
2 whole coriander plants, finely chopped (keep leaves separate, for garnish)
2 tablespoons dried shrimp, ground
2 tablespoons lemon juice
2 tablespoons sugar
1 tablespoon boiled water

Wrap shrimp paste in aluminium foil and dry-fry on each side for several minutes. Remove and, using a mortar and pestle, pound to a rough paste together with the garlic, 4 chillies, coriander roots and stems and the ground shrimp. Add the final chilli and pound lightly so it's slightly bruised but not mushy. Place in a serving bowl.

Pour in lemon juice, sugar and a tablespoon of boiled water, and stir. Taste to see if extra sugar or lemon juice is needed. Serve garnished with the reserved chopped coriander leaves.

Makes about 300 mL

1. Stir-fry onions and garlic and add prawns and meat pieces.

2. Push to one side, add beaten eggs and scramble.

3. Add cooked rice and stir-fry until heated through.

Thai Fried Rice — a delicious and nutritious meal on its own or a dish to feature at a Thai banquet.

STEAMED CHICKEN RICE
(KHAO MAN GAI)

4 tablespoons vegetable oil
4 cloves garlic
1 tablespoon chopped coriander root
1 teaspoon white pepper
4 chicken breasts, sliced into strips
400 g uncooked rice
1 litre chicken stock
sliced cucumber and chopped fresh
   coriander leaves, to garnish

In a heavy-based saucepan, stir-fry garlic in the vegetable oil until golden, then add coriander, pepper and chicken slices and stir-fry until chicken is cooked. Remove chicken and put aside but leave oily sauce in pan.

Add uncooked rice and stir-fry for 3–4 minutes. Pour in chicken stock and simmer slowly until liquid is level with the surface of the rice. Cover, turn off heat and allow to stand for 10 minutes.

When ready to serve, remove lid from rice, fluff it up with a fork and place on a serving dish in a mound. Cover with chicken slices and garnish with sliced cucumber and chopped coriander leaves. Serve with a spicy hot sauce.

Serves 4

SIMPLE FRIED RICE
(KHAO PAD TAMADA)

This is a sweet fried rice which is simple to make. It's ideal as a light snack, or as a bed for roast duck or roast pork pieces. Khao Pad Tamada literally means 'ordinary fried rice' and it's very common in Thailand, almost as common as the ingredient that gives it its colour, tomato sauce.

3 tablespoons vegetable oil
2 cloves garlic, finely chopped
1 medium-sized onion, finely chopped
3 tablespoons dried shrimp (soaked 5
   minutes, drained)
150 g any meat, cooked and cut into
   bite-sized pieces
4 tablespoons bottled tomato sauce
1 teaspoon sugar
pinch salt
500 g cooked rice (preferably chilled
   overnight)
2 eggs, lightly beaten
1 tomato, diced
½ capsicum, chopped
fresh coriander leaves, to garnish

Heat oil in large wok over medium heat and saute garlic and onion until garlic is golden. Add dried shrimp, meat pieces, tomato sauce, sugar and salt. Stir-fry for about 1 minute then add rice and stir well to combine.

Push rice to one side of wok, add a little more oil and pour in beaten egg. Allow to set slightly, then scramble. Stir egg through rice then add tomato and capsicum, stir several times and remove from heat. Garnish with chopped coriander leaves.

Serves 4

THAI FRIED RICE
(KHAO PAD)

This dish can be a meal in itself or the centrepiece to a dinner. Allow about 220 g cooked rice for each person.

5 tablespoons vegetable oil
3 medium-sized onions, finely chopped
3 cloves garlic, finely chopped
1 teaspoon sugar
1 tablespoon red curry paste or
   1 tablespoon bottled chilli or tabasco
   sauce
500 g cooked prawns (peeled), beef,
   pork, chicken or ham (any
   combination)
3 eggs, lightly beaten
880 g cooked rice (preferably cooked
   the day before and chilled)
2 tablespoons fish sauce
1 capsicum, sliced
50 g green beans, finely sliced
1 tomato, chopped
2 tablespoons chopped shallots
GARNISH
cucumber slices, chilli flowers, shallot
   curls or fresh coriander leaves

Heat oil in a large wok and over a medium heat stir-fry onions and garlic until garlic is golden. Add sugar and stir to dissolve; if using curry paste, add and stir-fry. Add prawns and meat pieces and combine well. Push to one side and, using a little more oil if necessary, add beaten eggs. Wait a few moments for them to set, then slightly scramble them.

Add rice and stir-fry until heated through. Sprinkle with chilli sauce, if using it, and fish sauce. Add capsicum, beans, tomato and shallots and stir-fry briefly to heat through. Don't overcook or make the rice gluggy.

Taste to see if extra fish sauce or a touch of sugar is needed. Remove and serve with garnishes of your choice.

Serves 4

STICKY RICE
(KHAO NIEO)

Sticky Rice can be eaten as an accompaniment to a main meal, or as a dessert with added coconut milk and fruit.

200 g glutinous (sticky) rice
water, for steaming

Rinse rice several times until water runs clear. Soak in water for 12 hours or overnight, then drain.

Line a saucepan steamer or bamboo basket with cheesecloth or similar fine-weave cotton cloth. Put rice in the steamer and steam for 45 minutes until rice is tender and translucent. Remove from heat and fluff up with a fork.

Serves 4

STEAMED RICE
(KHAO PLOW)

400 g long-grain rice
3½ cups (875 mL) water (depends on saucepan size)
little vegetable oil (optional)

Rinse rice in a colander, drain and place in a heavy-based saucepan with a tight-fitting lid. Add enough water to cover the rice by about 3 cm (the Thais call it about one knuckle length). If you like, add a few drops of vegetable oil and stir, so the rice doesn't stick to the bottom; don't add salt.

Bring to the boil and simmer rapidly until the water is level with the surface of the rice. When tunnels or bubbles appear on the top of the rice, cover tightly and turn the heat down to very low, or, if you have an electric hotplate, turn it off and leave the saucepan on the warm hot-plate. Don't remove the lid for at least 10 minutes, which is about the time needed for the rice to absorb all the water. Just before serving, remove the lid and fluff up the rice with a fork.

Serves 6

STEAM RICE IN YOUR MICROWAVE

Place the rice, with a knuckle length of tap water to cover it, in a ceramic casserole with a loosely fitting lid.

Cook covered, on high for about 12 minutes, then stand, still covered, for another 6 minutes. Times vary with this method, depending on microwave size and wattage. Check after 10 minutes on high, to see if the liquid has been absorbed.

Clockwise from left: Sticky rice, the most pearly white of these wholesome grains, is aromatic, slightly greasy to touch before it's cooked and needs lots of rinsing to remove all the starch; short-grain rice; and the most popular rice in Thailand today, long-grain rice. The Thais never salt their rice while it's cooking. They eat it unsalted.

CHIANG MAI NOODLES
(KHAO SOI CHIANG MAI)

165 mL vegetable oil
1 large onion, finely sliced
6 large cloves garlic, finely sliced
4 tablespoons red curry paste
500 g lean chicken or pork, finely
   chopped or minced
2 tablespoons sugar
3 tablespoons fish sauce
200 g (dried weight) egg noodles or
   spaghetti
4 tablespoons finely chopped shallots
4 tablespoons finely chopped fresh
   coriander
3 tablespoons dried chilli flakes
   soaked in 4 tablespoons warmed
   vinegar
4 tablespoons fish sauce mixed with 2
   tablespoons lemon juice

Fry onion in 1 tablespoon vegetable oil until golden. Remove, drain and set aside. In another tablespoon of oil, fry garlic until crisp and golden. Remove, drain and set aside.

In a wok or large frypan heat remaining ½ cup (125 mL) vegetable oil and stir-fry curry paste for a minute or so, then add chicken, sugar and fish sauce and stir-fry for several minutes. If chicken is very moist, allow the water to evaporate, frying over a hot flame so sauce remains oily. Turn off heat and set aside.

Bring 1.5–2 litres water to the boil in a large saucepan and cook noodles to desired tenderness, about 10 minutes, then drain. Reheat chicken in wok.

Serve noodles in individual bowls, covering them with chicken and sauce. Garnish with fried onion and garlic, fresh shallots and coriander. Serve with side bowls of dried chilli flakes soaked in warm vinegar, and fish sauce mixed with lemon juice.

Serves 4

Clockwise from left: Thick wet rice noodles, available fresh at Asian foodstores, are sold in folded sheets for you to slice into strips or squares. There are many varieties of dried noodles like the tangled threads of cellophane noodles made from mung-beans, rice-stick noodles and bundles of egg noodles.

Credit: Appley Hoare Antiques

THAI FRIED NOODLES
(PAD THAI)

This is a universal favourite among lovers of Thai food and in Thailand is a popular midday snack. It has become a signature dish at Thai restaurants around the world and varies enormously. If you don't have pork on hand, substitute chicken; even without the meat, the dish loses little of its appeal.

4 tablespoons vegetable oil
2 cloves garlic, finely chopped
100 g sliced raw pork
4 large green (uncooked) prawns,
    peeled, deveined, tails intact
1 tablespoon dried shrimp
2 tablespoons pickled white radish,
    finely chopped (optional)
50 g beancurd, diced
3 tablespoons lemon juice
3 tablespoons fish sauce
3 tablespoons sugar
150 g (dried weight) rice stick noodles
    (thicker ones preferably and soaked
    at least 15 minutes in warm water,
    then drained well)
2 eggs, beaten
50 g bean sprouts
3 tablespoons crushed peanuts
2 tablespoons chopped garlic chives or
    shallots
2 tablespoons chopped fresh coriander
    leaves
GARNISH
½ teaspoon roasted chilli powder or
    flakes (see recipe), optional
lemon or lime wedges

Heat oil in a wok and gently stir-fry garlic until golden. Add pork, increase heat and fry until cooked. Add prawns, dried shrimp and pickled radish and continue to stir-fry. Add beancurd, stir, reduce heat and add lemon juice, fish sauce and sugar, stirring to dissolve.

Add noodles and stir through the mixture briefly. Push to one side and, adding a little more oil if necessary, quickly add beaten eggs. Once they begin to set, gently scramble them, still keeping them to one side. Place most of the bean sprouts and a handful of crushed peanuts, garlic chives and coriander leaves on top of the noodles. Stir these with scrambled eggs through the noodles.

Serve on a large plate with little mounds of chilli flakes, the remaining bean sprouts, peanuts, garlic chives, coriander and the lemon wedges.

Serves 4

Two very popular everyday meals — Thai Fried Noodles and Fried Rice with Basil. Experiment, to vary them and to create your own signature versions like restaurants around the world have done.

FRIED RICE WITH BASIL
(KHAO PAD KRAPAO)

4 tablespoons vegetable oil
3 cloves garlic, finely chopped
1 tablespoon chopped fresh chilli
200 g fresh chicken, pork or prawns,
    cut into bite-sized pieces
500 g cooked rice, preferably chilled
    overnight
1 tablespoon sugar
1 tablespoon fish sauce
1 tablespoon soy sauce
2 tablespoons chopped shallots
4 tablespoons fresh basil leaves
1 tablespoon chopped fresh coriander

In a wok or frypan, stir-fry garlic in vegetable oil until golden, then add chilli and chicken and stir-fry until cooked.

Add cooked rice, sugar, fish and soy sauces and cook over medium heat, stirring and tossing gently. When mixture is well combined, stir through shallots, basil leaves and coriander, cook another minute, then serve.

Serves 4

ROASTED CHILLI POWDER OR FLAKES
(PRIK PAO, PRIK PON)

When recipes call for dried chilli powder or flakes, it's easy to make your own if you have a blender, spice grinder or food processor and some dried chillies.

100 g dried red chillies (also called
    small or party chillies)

Remove stems from chillies, then dry-fry or roast chillies in the oven at 200°C (400°F) until brown. Blend briefly if you want flakes, or process until they become a fine powder. Store in an airtight container.

Serve in a side bowl to sprinkle on noodle dishes, soups and salads, or mix one tablespoon chilli flakes with two tablespoons warm vinegar. Chilli flakes and vinegar make a fine condiment to go with noodle soups.

ROASTED CHILLI PASTE
(NAM PRIK PAO)

There are many variations of Roasted Chilli Paste. The traditional method requires the ashes of a fire to roast the garlic and onions until they're black. Here is an acceptable alternative.

There are several good quality commercial brands available in Asian food stores and these are acceptable substitutes. Otherwise, open the kitchen windows wide and prepare for a smoke out. The end result is worth it. This paste is an ingredient in several Thai dishes, the most famous ones being the Tom Yam soups. It can also be used as a condiment for rice, vegetables and salads, and is an interesting, if pungent, spread for toast. Use sparingly.

6 large cloves garlic, unpeeled
2 medium-sized onions, unpeeled
2 teaspoons shrimp paste
6 large dried red chillies
2 tablespoons ground dried shrimp
3 tablespoons brown sugar
2 teaspoons tamarind concentrate
    mixed with 2 tablespoons hot water
2 tablespoons vegetable oil, for frying

In a heavy-based iron pan, dry-fry the unpeeled garlic and onions over a fierce heat until they're charred. Cool, discard skins, and chop them roughly.

Wrap the shrimp paste in aluminium foil and dry-fry in same pan for several minutes on each side. Cool and unwrap. Process all ingredients except oil for frying into a smooth paste, in a food processor, blender or mortar. If necessary, add 1 tablespoon vegetable oil to help bind ingredients together.

Fry resulting paste in 2 tablespoons oil in a saucepan, gently stirring so paste doesn't catch or burn. Taste to see if extra tamarind juice, sugar or any salt is required to balance flavours. Cook for several minutes, then cool and place in a sterilised jar with a tightly fitting lid. This paste keeps for several months refrigerated.

Makes about 200 mL

THAI CURRY PASTES

The first sound of the morning throughout much of Thailand is a dull, rhythmic thump — the pounding of wooden pestle on granite mortar. The day's curry pastes are being prepared.

A mixture of dry spices and fresh herbs, the pastes are usually combined with coconut milk, citrus leaves, chillies and a small proportion of meat or vegetables. The creamy rich curry sauces are eaten with lots of steamed rice, balancing the meal and alleviating the pain of searing hot chillies.

An inexpensive Thai mortar and pestle and some ingredients for making your own authentic Thai curry pastes — onions, limes, dried red chillies, dried galangal, fresh hot green chillies, cinnamon sticks, fresh lemon grass, coriander seeds, cloves, peppercorns, ground coriander, garlic, cumin seeds, cardamom pods, fresh coriander roots and shrimp paste.

GREEN CURRY PASTE
(KRUANG GAENG KEOW WAN)

4 tablespoons roughly chopped lemon
   grass
1 tablespoon galangal, presoaked for
   30 minutes
2 tablespoons chopped garlic
1 medium-sized onion, chopped
2 whole coriander plants, including
   roots and stems, chopped
1 teaspoon chopped lime or lemon zest
15 fresh green chillies
10 black peppercorns, cracked
2 teaspoons ground coriander
2 teaspoons ground cumin
2 teaspoons shrimp paste
1 teaspoon salt
3 cloves
3 bay leaves
2 tablespoons vegetable oil, for
   blending

Blend or process all the ingredients
together, using extra oil if necessary to
achieve a smooth paste.

This recipe makes about 1 cup
(250 mL) of paste, and we suggest you
store half of it in a clean jar in the refrigerator, where it will last for several weeks.
Freeze the remainder in pre-measured
amounts for later use. Most curries
require about 1–2 tablespoons.

Makes 1 cup (250 mL)

RED CURRY PASTE
(KRUANG GAENG PED)

15 medium-sized dried red chillies
10 black peppercorns
1 tablespoon ground coriander
1 tablespoon ground cumin
1 teaspoon salt
4 whole cloves
3 bay leaves
1 teaspoon ground nutmeg
1 medium-sized onion, chopped
2 tablespoons chopped garlic
4 tablespoons roughly chopped lemon
   grass
1 tablespoon galangal, soaked ½ hour
   in hot water
4 tablespoons chopped coriander roots
2 teaspoons chopped lime zest
2 teaspoons shrimp paste
2 tablespoons vegetable oil, for
   blending

Grind the first eight ingredients in a
blender or spice mill. Combine with
remaining ingredients in a food
processor. If using a mortar and pestle it
will take about an hour to pound ingredients to a smooth paste (with a few rests
included). Good quality red curry paste
can also be found in Asian foodstores.

When you've made a smooth reddish
brown paste, refrigerate half of it in a
clean tightly lidded jar, and freeze the
rest in pre-measured amounts, of about
1½ tablespoons each.

Makes about 300 mL

MUSSAMAN (MUSLIM) CURRY PASTE
(KRUANG GAENG MUSSAMAN)

8 large dried red chillies, stems
   removed
5 cloves
2 teaspoons ground cinnamon or
   1 stick
6 cardamom seeds or 3 cardamom
   pods
½ teaspoon ground or grated nutmeg
3 bay leaves
1 tablespoon coriander, ground or in
   seeds
1 tablespoon cumin, ground or in
   seeds
1 teaspoon shrimp paste
2 teaspoons galangal, soaked and
   sliced
2 tablespoons chopped lemon grass
2 medium-sized onions, chopped
4 cloves garlic, chopped

Dry-fry or roast chillies, cloves, cinnamon, cardamom, nutmeg, bay leaves,
coriander and cumin, to release their
flavours. Don't burn or char them. Place
them in a blender or spice mill and grind
to a coarse powder.

Combine with remaining ingredients
and make a smooth paste either with a
mortar and pestle or in a food processor
or blender, using a little vegetable oil if
necessary to blend.

Place in a sterilised, tightly capped jar.
It will keep in the refrigerator for a few
weeks, or you can freeze pre-measured
amounts.

Makes about 1½ cups (375 mL)

TOM YAMS AND OTHER THAI SOUPS

After rice, soups are the mainstay of the Thai diet. They range from the humble rice soup, khao tom, to the queen of the Thai soups, the tom yam, of which Tom Yam Goong — Spicy Prawn Soup — is the most regal.

SPICY PRAWN SOUP
(TOM YAM GOONG)

This delicious soup is the most famous of the tom yam Thai soups, and in Thailand is often served in a charcoal-heated steamboat. Tom yam goong is made with prawns and if you like it hot then include fresh chillies. If there's any doubt, serve it with a side dish of chilli. Tom yams can also be made with pork, beef, chicken or fish, and for a really special meal, why not Tom Yam Talay — Spicy Soup with Mixed Seafood. When using seafood ingredients, use a stock made from prawn shells instead of chicken stock, and add some lemon grass and citrus leaves.

1.5 litres chicken Thai Soup Stock (see recipe)
8 pieces galangal
8 dried Kaffir lime leaves
2 tablespoons lemon grass, cut in 2 cm pieces
4 tablespoons lemon juice
1 tablespoon fish sauce
1 tablespoon roasted chilli paste, bought or homemade (see recipe)
16 medium-sized fresh green (uncooked) prawns, peeled, deveined, tails intact
20 champignons, sliced in half
2 small fresh chillies, finely sliced
chopped fresh coriander leaves

Bring chicken stock to the boil, add galangal, lime leaves and lemon grass and boil rapidly for several minutes. Turn down heat to low and add lemon juice, fish sauce and roasted chilli paste, stir and simmer for another minute.

Add prawns and mushrooms and cook another 3 minutes, being careful not to overcook the prawns. Taste to see if extra lemon juice, fish sauce or roasted chilli paste is needed. Add sliced chillies, if using. Serve garnished with chopped coriander leaves.

Serves 4

SPICY CHICKEN SOUP
(TOM YAM GAI)
— as above, replacing prawns with 300 g chicken fillets, cut into bite-sized pieces.

SPICY PORK SOUP
(TOM YAM MU),
AND SPICY BEEF SOUP
(TOM YAM NUA)
— as above, replacing prawns with 200 g sliced meat strips.

STUFFED CUCUMBER SOUP
(GAENG CHUD THANG KWA SOD SAI)

300 g pork, roughly chopped
½ small onion, finely chopped
2 large cloves garlic, finely chopped
1 teaspoon pepper
1 teaspoon sugar
2 tablespoons fish sauce
3 medium-sized cucumbers
2 litres pork or chicken Thai Soup Stock (see recipe)

Process pork, onion, garlic, pepper, sugar and fish sauce in a food processor until you have a fine-textured filling. Peel cucumbers, leaving some strips of green for colour. Cut ends off each cucumber then cut each into three equal pieces. Hollow out ready for filling. Fill with stuffing mixture and secure with toothpicks, placed crossways, at both ends.

Heat stock in a large saucepan. Gently place stuffed cucumbers in the stock and simmer them slowly for about 5 minutes. This recipe allows for two pieces per person, if serving four people. Taste to see whether broth needs extra pepper, sugar or fish sauce. Remove from heat and serve.

Serves 4

Spicy Prawn Soup and Stuffed Cucumber Soup.

Credit: Dansab; Appley Hoare Antiques

THAI SOUP STOCK
(NAM GAENG CHUD)

It's always a good idea to have at least one easy and nutritious soup on hand for an impromptu meal and, for that, frozen stock in the freezer is a necessity. Here's a recipe for basic soup stock which you can adapt for beef, chicken, pork or seafood. Chicken is the most versatile stock, as it can be used as a base for any soup, even seafood.

2.25 litres water
600 g chicken bones (or pork, beef or fish)
2 stalks celery, chopped
2 medium-sized onions, quartered
2 coriander roots, roughly chopped
4 dried Kaffir lime leaves
1 tablespoon chopped fresh ginger root
salt and pepper

Bring all ingredients to the boil in a large saucepan and cook for several minutes on high; reduce heat and skim fat from the surface. Cover and simmer gently for about an hour.

Strain, several times if necessary, through a fine sieve to achieve as clear a stock as possible. Refrigerate, then remove any fat from the surface once again. The stock will keep in the refrigerator for several days or can be frozen for long-term storages.

Makes 1.5–2 litres

SOUP STOCKS

Recipes in this book usually specify Thai Soup Stock (see recipe above). This is a very versatile basic stock, which can be adapted as required to use chicken, beef, pork or seafood.

If you are in a hurry, however, and have leftover stock from another recipe, you can substitute this instead of making up a fresh batch of Thai Soup Stock.

A useful habit is to make up more stock than you need for a recipe, and freeze the leftovers in ice cube form.

SPICY CHICKEN, COCONUT AND GALANGAL SOUP
(TOM KAH GAI)

1 litre coconut milk
6 dried Kaffir lime leaves
3 pieces dried galangal or
   2 teaspoons powdered galangal
1 tablespoon lemon juice
2 tablespoons fish sauce
1 teaspoon sugar
2 teaspoons roasted chilli paste or
   1 teaspoon sliced fresh chilli
1 tablespoon lemon grass, sliced into 2 cm pieces
200 g chicken breast, fillet or thigh, cut into bite-sized pieces
100 g champignons, fresh or canned
fresh coriander, mint or basil leaves, to garnish

In a saucepan, bring coconut milk to the boil, add lime leaves, galangal, lemon juice, fish sauce, sugar, roasted chilli paste and lemon grass. Simmer for 5 minutes.

Add chicken and mushrooms and simmer another 5 minutes. Taste to see if extra lemon juice, fish sauce or sugar is needed. If soup is too thick, add a little more coconut milk or water. Pour into serving bowls and garnish with fresh coriander leaves, mint or basil.

Serves 4

VEGETABLE AND PRAWN SOUP
(GAENG LIANG)

1 tablespoon dried shrimp
3 medium-sized onions, chopped
10 peppercorns, cracked
1.5 litres chicken Thai Soup Stock (see recipe)
2 tablespoons fish sauce
4 medium-sized carrots, sliced
60 g cauliflower florets
2 zucchini, sliced
30 g sliced green beans
12 large green (uncooked) prawns, peeled, deveined, tails intact
fresh basil leaves, to garnish

Pound or blend in a food processor with a little water, the dried shrimp, onions and peppercorns. Bring stock to the boil in a saucepan, then add fish sauce and the paste you've just made and simmer for several minutes.

Add vegetables, the softer ones last, and simmer another minute or two. Add prawns and simmer until they are pink and just cooked and the vegetables are tender, about 3–4 minutes. Remove from heat and pour into serving bowls. Garnish with basil leaves.

Serves 4

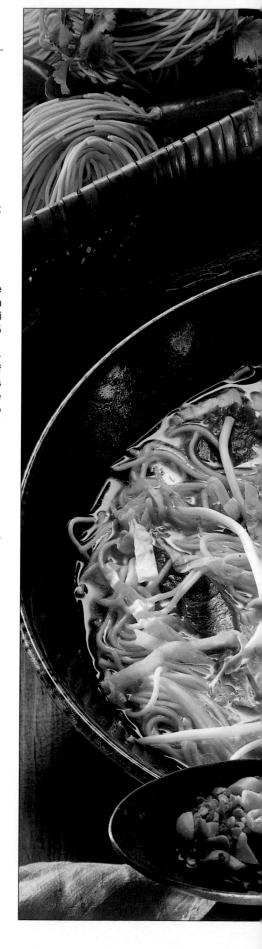

PORK AND NOODLE SOUP
(BA MEE NAM MUU)

This is a very popular soup eaten at any time of the day in Thailand, beside roadside vendors and at the open shop fronts of Thai 'soup-kitchens'. The soup can be served with any type of noodle, rice or egg, wide or narrow. For this recipe we've chosen Chinese egg noodles. It can be served at home as a hearty curtain-raiser to a Thai banquet or as a light meal in itself.

2 litres chicken Thai Soup Stock (see recipe)
250 g Roast Red Pork (see recipe) or any cooked lean pork, cut into thin slices
1 tablespoon sugar
2 tablespoons fish sauce
150 g Chinese dried egg noodles
4 cloves garlic, finely chopped and fried until crisp
50 g bean sprouts
3 lettuce leaves, shredded
GARNISH
2 tablespoons chopped fresh coriander leaves
1 tablespoon dried red chilli flakes or fresh chillies, seeded and sliced
2 shallots, finely chopped
2 tablespoons roughly ground roasted peanuts

In a large saucepan bring chicken stock to the boil, then add pork, sugar and fish sauce. Lower heat, add noodles and simmer them until just tender, about 5 minutes.

Add fried garlic, bean sprouts and shredded lettuce. Immediately remove from heat and pour into a large tureen or serving bowl. Garnish with coriander leaves then put the rest of the garnishes in bowls and let people help themselves.

Serves 4

Pork and Noodle Soup can be made with any type of noodle, rice or egg, wide or narrow.

PUMPKIN AND COCONUT CREAM SOUP
(GAENG LIANG FAK TONG)

400 g pumpkin, peeled and cut in 2 cm cubes
1 tablespoon lemon or lime juice
100 g green (uncooked) prawns or dried shrimp
2 medium-sized onions
¼ teaspoon shrimp paste
2 fresh chillies, seeded or 2 teaspoons roasted chilli paste (optional)
1 tablespoon finely chopped lemon grass
300 mL water
3 cups (750 mL) coconut milk (reserve thick cream from top)
1 tablespoon fish sauce
1 teaspoon sugar
½ teaspoon pepper
80 g fresh basil leaves, reserving some for garnish

Sprinkle pumpkin with lemon juice and let it stand for about 20 minutes. Shell and devein fresh prawns or wash dried shrimp.

In a food processor, combine prawns, onions, shrimp paste, chillies, lemon grass and a little water, and blend to a smooth paste.

Combine 300 mL water with thin coconut milk in a large saucepan and stir in the paste, fish sauce, sugar and pepper.

Bring to the boil, then reduce heat and stir with a wooden spoon to ensure a smooth consistency. Add pumpkin and simmer gently for about 20 minutes until pumpkin is tender. Taste to see if extra seasoning is required.

Just before serving, stir in basil leaves and reserved thick coconut cream. Garnish with a sprinkle of extra basil leaves.

Serves 4

Pumpkin and Coconut Cream Soup can be served in a large pumpkin shell.

Rice Soup with Chicken is a mild soup that makes a perfect late-night supper.

RICE SOUP WITH CHICKEN
(KHAO TOM GAI)

The famous Asian cure-all, Khao Tom, or Rice Soup can be made with chicken, pork or seafood pieces. It's a mild soup eaten by the Thais at breakfast or any time of the day if they're feeling off colour. It's a great antidote for hang-overs, and a fine late-night supper.

100 g uncooked rice
1 tablespoon vegetable oil
1 tablespoon chopped garlic
1 tablespoon finely sliced fresh ginger root
200 g lean chicken, cut into bite-sized pieces (see Note)
1 teaspoon white pepper
3 tablespoons fish sauce
2 tablespoons sliced onion
1 tablespoon chopped fresh coriander
1 tablespoon chopped shallots
GARNISH
crispy fried noodles, fresh herb leaves, sliced chillies or capsicum, chopped shallots

Rinse rice several times, then place in saucepan with 2 litres water and bring to boil. Simmer slowly adding a little more water if necessary so rice becomes like porridge and there is plenty of rice stock for soup. You need about 1.5 litres of stock.

In another large saucepan, heat oil and stir-fry garlic and ginger, then add chicken, pepper and fish sauce. Stir-fry until chicken is cooked, then add onion, rice and rice stock, stirring well, and cook for another few minutes.

Just before serving, stir in chopped coriander and shallots and add garnishes of your choice.

Serves 4–6

Note: Other suggested alternatives to chicken for Khao Tom include fresh prawns, fish pieces, liver strips, duck, Roast Red Pork (see recipe) and roast duck pieces.

BEEF NOODLE SOUP
(GWAYTIO NUA)

This soup is particularly good when made with Rich Beef Stock (see recipe). Otherwise any beef, chicken or pork stock will do.

1 litre Rich Beef Stock (see recipe)
4 cloves garlic, chopped
1 stalk celery, sliced
2 onions, sliced
6 dried mushrooms, soaked, stems removed, sliced
2 tablespoons fish sauce
1 tablespoon soy sauce
1 teaspoon ground black pepper
250 g lean beef or liver, cut into strips
300 g fresh gwaytio (rice) noodles, cut into strips or 150 g (dried weight) rice vermicelli, soaked 15 minutes then drained
2 shallots, chopped

GARNISH
coriander leaves, chopped shallots, celery, bean sprouts, mint and chilli flakes or Chilli Vinegar with Garlic and Ginger (see recipe)

Heat stock in a large soup pot then add the garlic, celery, onions, dried mushrooms, fish sauce, soy sauce and pepper. Bring to the boil then reduce heat and simmer for about 5 minutes. Increase the heat again and boil rapidly.

Place beef strips in a straining-spoon or strainer and hold in the boiling stock for no more than 1 minute. Remove and drain.

Reduce heat, remove any scum from the surface and add the noodles. Simmer another 2 minutes, stirring to separate. Stir in the shallots, then remove soup from heat.

Serve sprinkled with coriander leaves, in a large tureen. Place bowls of garnishes and the meat strips on the table and have people help themselves to the soup and garnishes of their choice.

The Thais usually have a bowl of chilli flakes in warmed vinegar on the table for Beef Noodle Soup, but the best condiment to serve is Chilli Vinegar with Garlic and Ginger (see recipe).

Serves 4

Beef, and Other Main Meat Dishes

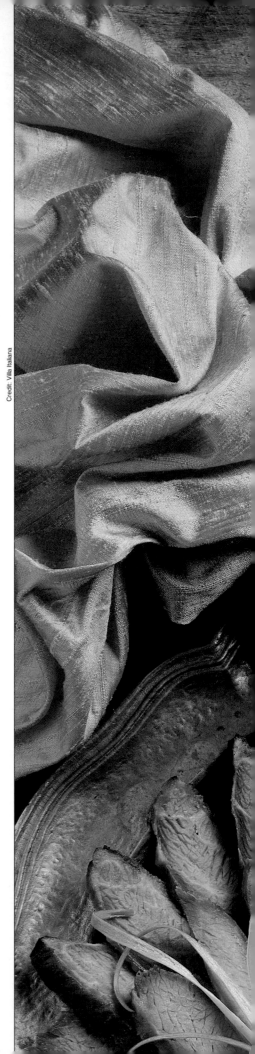

Main meals of beef and other meats are reserved for special occasions in Thailand, usually family celebrations or festivals. For the majority of people, meat is expensive, so the basic Thai diet remains fish and rice.

On an average day, Thais are more likely to eat small quantities of meat as a secondary ingredient in soups, noodles, curries and salads, using the meat to flavour the dish, rather than as a major source of protein.

ROAST RED PORK
(MUU DAENG)

Roast red pork hangs invitingly in the shop windows of Chinese delicatessens together with roasted whole ducks and chickens. By the kilogram, it's almost cheaper to buy it ready roasted, but here's a recipe for the Chinese delicacy, muu daeng, which is now often eaten by the Thais. They snack on muu daeng pieces, finely slice it and add it to a variety of stir-fried rice or vegetable dishes, or serve it as a simple meal with plain rice.

1 kg pork fillets or pork loin with bone and rind removed
½ teaspoon red food colouring, mixed with 3 tablespoons water
coriander sprigs or shallot curls, to garnish
MARINADE
1 tablespoon fish sauce
1 tablespoon soy sauce
2 tablespoons Hoisin sauce
1 tablespoon cooking sherry
1 tablespoon sugar
1 tablespoon grated fresh ginger root
3 cloves garlic, chopped
½ teaspoon Chinese Five Spice Powder
1 tablespoon sesame oil
½ teaspoon ground fennel or fennel seeds, or 3 star anise, crushed

Trim the pork of fat. Wearing rubber gloves, rub it with the red food colouring mixture, or put pork in a plastic bag with the food colouring and cover it that way, otherwise you'll end up with red hands. Put pork aside.

In a blender or food processor, combine marinade ingredients to a smooth paste. Cover pork with it, again wearing rubber gloves, and let meat stand for at least 2 hours, preferably overnight.

Preheat oven to 230°C (450°F). Place pork on a rack in a baking dish, reserving marinade for basting. Cook pork for 10 minutes, baste with marinade, then lower heat to 180°C (350°F). Roast for about 1 hour, basting occasionally. Remove from oven and let stand for at least 15 minutes before slicing.

Serve either warm, sliced thinly, arranged on a flat dish and garnished with coriander, or let it cool whole, for later use. It can then be cut into slices, strips or cubes and added to stir-fry dishes or soups.

Serves 4

STIR-FRIED BEEF WITH BROCCOLI
(PAK PAD GUP NUA)

3 tablespoons vegetable oil
3 cloves garlic, finely chopped
200 g lean beef, thinly sliced into strips
1 tablespoon oyster sauce
1 tablespoon fish sauce
1 teaspoon sugar
500 g broccoli (preferably Asian), cut diagonally into 2.5 cm pieces (see Note)

In a wok over medium heat, stir-fry garlic in oil until golden. Add beef and stir-fry for several minutes, reduce heat and stir in oyster and fish sauces and sugar. Cook until sugar dissolves, then add broccoli, stir and cover for several minutes until cooked. If necessary, add a little water or stock to help steam. Serve with rice.

Serves 4

Note: Bok choy, spinach or green beans can be substituted.

Stir-fried Beef with Broccoli and Roast Red Pork.

1. *Shape beef mince into small round balls and roll in flour.*

2. *Fry beef balls until brown.*

3. *Make sauce with curry paste, coconut milk, fish sauce and peanuts.*

4. *Add meatballs to sauce and simmer.*

PANANG BEEF BALLS
(PANANG NUA)

500 g lean beef, minced
½ cup (60 g) flour
3 tablespoons vegetable oil
2 tablespoons red curry paste, bought or homemade (see recipe)
about 1½ cups (350 mL) coconut milk
1½ tablespoons fish sauce
2 tablespoons ground peanuts or crunchy peanut butter
1 tablespoon sugar
2 tablespoons chopped fresh basil or mint leaves, to garnish

Shape beef mince into small round balls about 2.5 cm in diameter. Roll balls in flour, dusting off excess. Heat oil in a wok and fry beef balls until brown, tilting and rocking wok so balls fry evenly. Remove and set aside on absorbent kitchen paper.

In remaining oil, stir-fry red curry paste for several minutes over low heat to prevent sticking. Add coconut milk, stir, then add fish sauce, peanuts and sugar. Taste to see if extra fish sauce or sugar is needed, then return beef balls to sauce and simmer for about 5 minutes. Garnish with chopped basil leaves and serve with rice or a salad.

Serves 4

RICH BEEF STOCK
(NAM TOM HAANG WOOA)

This soup stock can be made with any meaty beef bones but is particularly tasty when made with oxtail. It provides you with more than a litre of stock (or more if you decide to use extra oxtail and water), and also forms the basis for a traditional Thai casserole. For those who like oxtail — that rather humble part of the cow now finding its way onto some of the best restaurant menus — try Thai Oxtail Casserole (Tom Haang Wooa).

500 g oxtail or meaty beef bones
1 large onion, sliced
2 large stalks celery with leaves, roughly chopped
6 small whole coriander plants with roots, roughly chopped
2 large stalks lemon grass, chopped
6 large cloves garlic, finely chopped
1 cinnamon stick
2 star anise
½ cup (125 g) sugar
about ½ cup (100 mL) thin soy sauce
1 tablespoon black peppercorns
water

Place all ingredients in a large soup pot with enough water to cover the oxtail by about 12 cm, and simmer slowly for at least 3 hours. Check water level occasionally and continue to top up, so you finish with about 1.5 litres of stock.

Taste to see if extra seasoning is required. There should be a balance of spicy and sweet flavours.

When oxtail meat is soft, remove and set aside. Allow stock to cool then refrigerate for an hour or so, or overnight. Skim fat from surface and pour stock through cotton or cheesecloth, reserving all the bits and pieces. Wrap them in the cloth to form a little bundle like a bouquet garni. Discard or use it with the oxtail for Thai Oxtail Casserole (see recipe). Freeze your rich beef stock for later use.

Makes 1.5 litres

THAI OXTAIL CASSEROLE
(TOM HAANG WOOA)

500 g cooked oxtail, 4 cups Stock and Thai 'bouquet garni' from Rich Beef Stock (see recipe)
1 large onion, sliced
3 cooked potatoes, quartered
3 tomatoes, diced
50 g sliced green beans or similar vegetable
3 tablespoons bean shoots (optional)
GARNISH
3 tablespoons chopped fresh coriander and 3 tablespoons chopped shallots

Place cooked oxtail in a large saucepan with Rich Beef Stock, and a little extra water if necessary to almost cover oxtail. Bring to the boil and drop in Thai 'bouquet garni'. Simmer for 10 minutes or until gravy is the consistency you want.

Add onion, cooked potatoes and tomatoes and simmer another few minutes so they retain their own flavours. Just before serving add beans and cook until they are just tender.

Remove 'bouquet garni', and stir through bean shoots if using them. Serve sprinkled with coriander leaves and chopped shallots with a side dish of rice or noodles, and a sauce of your choice.

Serves 4

SALTY SUN-DRIED BEEF
(NUA KEM)

This is a traditional favourite in Thailand, but one that's unusual by Western standards. It's usually served as an accompaniment to curries as the saltiness counteracts their hot spiciness. It's common in Thailand to see beef fillets hanging from the balcony or on a fencepost within sight of the kitchen. The meat which has been well salted overnight is drying in the sun, and the only danger of it 'going off' results from birds occasionally flying off with it.

1 kg lean beef (large 2.5 cm steaks)
5 tablespoons coarse salt
vegetable oil, for deep-frying

Rub steak fillets well with salt, then stack in layers in a covered bowl and leave overnight in the refrigerator.

If you want to, you can dry the meat further in the sun for several hours either side. If there is no sun that day, or you'd rather not be too traditional, you can simply drain the meat after it has been well salted, and cook. The 'integrity' of the dish won't suffer too much.

Fry the steak in hot oil so meat becomes crispy golden on the outside. Then cool and slice across the grain into fine slices about 2.5 cm wide. Serve warm or at room temperature, with a curry dish.

Serves 4

Panang Beef Balls garnished with strips of fresh basil leaves.

35

EASY STIR-FRYING STEPS

Stir-frying is one of the easiest cooking methods to master. It's fast, ensuring your food tastes fresh and delicious.

Hot oil seals the outside of the food, locking both moisture and flavour inside. Meat and fish are tender and juicy; vegetables stay crisp and crunchy, retaining their vitamins and enjoyable texture; fresh herbs are often added last, stirred to heat through and release their flavours.

STIR-FRIED BEEF WITH GINGER, ONION, CAPSICUM AND SHALLOTS
(PAD KING NUA)

2 tablespoons vegetable oil
1 clove garlic, finely chopped
1 tablespoon sliced ginger root, cut into fine strips
200 g lean beef strips
1 tablespoon oyster sauce
1 tablespoon fish sauce
1 teaspoon pickled soy bean (optional)
½ teaspoon sugar
pinch white pepper
3 tablespoons stock or water (optional)
2 shallots, sliced into 2 cm lengths
1 onion, sliced
½ red capsicum, cut in strips
3 tablespoons dried wood fungus, soaked for 1 hour, cores removed or fresh mushrooms
fresh coriander leaves, to garnish

Heat oil in wok or frypan and stir-fry garlic and ginger over medium heat until golden. Add beef, oyster and fish sauces and pickled soy bean and slowly stir-fry for 2–3 minutes.

Add sugar and pepper and taste for a balance of sweet and salty flavours. If required, add a few tablespoons of stock or water to give a good residue of gravy.

Stir in shallots, onion, capsicum and wood fungus and stir-fry for another 1–2 minutes. Remove, garnish with fresh coriander leaves and serve with rice.

Serves 4

1. Preparation is the key to successful stir-frying. All ingredients must be attractively sliced to size before you start cooking. Vary the thickness of the slice depending on the density of the vegetable. For example thinner vegetables such as cabbage or spinach are sliced in larger pieces than carrots so that everything is cooked to perfection at the same time.

2. Heat oil in wok and stir-fry garlic and ginger over medium heat until golden. Add meat and sauces and slowly stir-fry for 2–3 minutes.

3. Stir-fry vegetables 1–2 minutes.

4. Garnish with fresh coriander leaves and serve with rice.

STIR-FRIED PORK AND GREEN BEANS
(MUU PAD TUA FAK YAW)

2 tablespoons vegetable oil
2 cloves garlic, finely chopped
250 g lean pork, sliced thinly then cut
  into bite-sized pieces
1½ tablespoons fish sauce
1 tablespoon oyster sauce
½ teaspoon pepper
1 teaspoon sugar
150–200 g green, preferably snake,
  beans, cut in 2.5 cm slices
3 tablespoons water or stock (optional)

Stir-fry garlic in vegetable oil in wok or
frypan. Add pork and stir-fry until golden.
Then add fish and oyster sauces, pepper
and sugar. Stir several times and add
beans. Stir-fry for 1 minute, adding a little
water or stock if necessary to keep a
good residue of gravy. Taste to see if
extra seasoning is required, and check
that pork is cooked. Remove from heat
and serve with rice.

Serves 4

CHILLI BEEF
(NUA PAD PRIK)

2 teaspoons vegetable oil
1 small clove garlic, finely chopped
1 teaspoon chopped fresh chilli
200 g lean beef, sliced into fine strips
1 teaspoon fish sauce
½ teaspoon oyster sauce
pinch salt
3 tablespoons Thai Soup Stock (see
  recipe) or water
3 tablespoons chopped shallots
3 tablespoons finely sliced capsicum
1 tablespoon basil leaves

In a wok or frypan, stir-fry garlic in oil until
golden, then add chilli. Cook for about 1
minute. Add beef, fish and oyster sauces
and salt, stirring slowly.

Pour in stock and simmer meat for several minutes until tender. Stir through
shallots, capsicum and basil and stir-fry
for about 30 seconds. Remove from heat
and serve with rice.

Serves 4

LAMB WITH CHILLI AND MINT
(NUA GAE PAD PRIK BAI SALANAI)

3 tablespoons vegetable oil
200 g lean lamb, cut in fine strips
1 clove garlic, finely chopped
1 tablespoon oyster sauce
1 tablespoon fish sauce
pinch sugar
1 tablespoon finely sliced fresh chilli
4–5 tablespoons fresh mint leaves,
  sliced if large

Heat oil in wok or frypan, and stir-fry lamb
for several minutes until almost cooked.
Add garlic, oyster and fish sauces, sugar
and chilli and stir-fry another 1–2 minutes. Taste to see if extra seasoning is
required — chilli, sugar or sauces.

When meat is cooked and tender, stir
mint leaves through, then remove from
heat. Serve with rice.

Serves 4

RED PORK CURRY
(GAENG PED MUU)

3 tablespoons vegetable oil
3 tablespoons red curry paste, bought
  or homemade (see recipe)
2 cups (500 mL) coconut milk
1 teaspoon dried Kaffir lime leaves,
  soaked for 10 minutes and sliced
500 g lean pork, sliced
1 teaspoon sugar
2 tablespoons fish sauce
50 g bamboo shoots or 100 g zucchini,
  eggplant or beans
1 tablespoon chopped basil leaves

In a wok or saucepan, stir-fry curry paste
into the vegetable oil over a medium heat
for several minutes. Add ½ cup
(125 mL) coconut milk and the lime
leaves and simmer for several minutes,
stirring frequently.

Add pork and cook for about 5 minutes, until moisture evaporates out of
pork and the sauce starts to thicken
again. Pour in remaining coconut milk,
sugar and fish sauce and simmer until
pork is cooked.

Taste to see if extra sugar, fish sauce
or perhaps some fresh chilli is needed.
The sauce should taste hot, spicy and
sweet. Add the vegetables a few minutes
before serving, cook for another minute
and remove from heat. Stir in the basil
leaves and serve with rice.

Serves 4

*Stir-fried Pork and Green Beans — Thais
often use snake beans for this recipe.*

SWEET AND SOUR PORK SPARE RIBS
(PREOW WAN GRADUK MUU)

600 g pork spare ribs
2 tablespoons fish sauce
fresh coriander leaves, to garnish

SAUCE
2 tablespoons vegetable oil
1 teaspoon chopped garlic
1 small onion, chopped
2 tablespoons sugar
2 teaspoons lemon juice
1 tablespoon fish sauce
1 tablespoon oyster sauce
½ cup (125 mL) bottled tomato sauce
2 tablespoons diced fresh pineapple
¼ teaspoon chopped fresh chilli
(optional)

Place spare ribs in a large saucepan, cover with water and simmer until tender, about 20 minutes. Drain, cool and rub lightly with salt. Allow them to stand for 3 hours — this can be done previous day. Barbecue or grill under a fierce heat until golden, but don't let them burn or catch. Drain and set aside.

To make the sauce, in a wok over a medium heat stir-fry garlic and onion in oil until golden. Add sugar, lemon juice and fish sauce, stir, then add oyster sauce, tomato sauce, pineapple and chilli, if using. Stir-fry until the mixture becomes a golden brown syrup.

Remove from heat and add pork spare ribs, one by one, covering them all with warm syrup. If necessary add a little more water to the mixture so that it covers ribs. Return to heat to simmer for just a minute or so, for ribs to absorb the full flavour of the sauce — don't let ribs make sauce too cloudy by overcooking or stirring.

Remove from heat, spoon into a serving dish and garnish with coriander leaves. Serve with rice.

Serves 4

MARINATED BRAISED BEEF WITH CUCUMBER
(NUA OB)

1 kg lean beef (large 2.5 cm thick
steaks)
1 tablespoon vegetable oil
¾ cup (185 mL) water
1 medium-sized cucumber, peeled and
finely sliced, or 1 Chinese lettuce,
sliced
1.5 cm piece fresh ginger root
fresh coriander leaves, to garnish

MARINADE
4 tablespoons soy sauce
2 tablespoons vegetable oil
6 coriander roots
3 tablespoons ground black pepper
1 tablespoon sugar

Marinated Braised Beef with Cucumber

Combine marinade ingredients in a blender and process to a smooth paste. Smear beef with paste and marinate for at least 10 minutes.

Smear a wok or frypan with oil and sear marinated beef. Add water and braise briefly until medium-rare. Remove beef and, if preparing in advance, cover with foil and reserve the sauce.

Just before serving, slice beef finely and arrange warm or cool beef on a bed of sliced cucumber or Chinese lettuce. Simmer reserved sauce and add ginger (either the whole piece, which can be discarded before serving, or finely chopped). More soy sauce, sugar or water can be added if required. Pour sauce over beef and cucumber and serve garnished with fresh coriander leaves.

Serves 4

GARLIC LAMB
(NUA GAE TOD GRATEUM)

150–200 g chopped green vegetable
e.g. leeks, spinach or zucchini
3 tablespoons vegetable oil
200 g lean lamb, sliced thinly
4 cloves garlic, finely chopped
½ teaspoon white pepper
½ teaspoon sugar
1 tablespoon fish sauce
1 tablespoon oyster sauce
fresh sprigs mint or coriander, to
garnish

Blanch prepared greens in boiling water for 1 minute. Drain, then place on serving dish.

Heat oil in wok or frypan and stir-fry lamb until nearly cooked, usually only a few minutes. Add garlic, pepper, sugar, fish and oyster sauces and stir-fry until lamb is completely cooked and tender.

Pour lamb and sauce over the greens and serve with rice. Garnish with mint or coriander sprigs.

Serves 4

SWEET PORK
(MUU WAN)

Traditionally, sweet pork is the Thai equivalent of ham, and was made to last a few days without refrigeration. Reboiled, it could be used for several meals, stir-fried or eaten cold. We don't suggest you do that, but it can be cooked, then refrigerated and served cold as an appetiser with spicy sauce dip, or served hot with rice. Any pork can be used, but preferably choose meat that's moist — for instance, a whole loin of pork, or spare ribs cut into 5 cm pieces.

½ cup (125 g) sugar
2 cups (500 mL) water
750 g loin of pork or spare ribs, trimmed of excess fat
2–3 large onions, chopped
1 tablespoon salt

In a large saucepan over medium heat, caramelise sugar and water until golden brown, being careful not to burn, then place pork, either whole or in pieces, into the pan. Smear it with syrup and brown for several minutes on all sides.

Add onion and brown, lower heat, cover pork with extra water and stir in salt. Simmer for about 1 hour for a large piece, less for ribs or smaller pieces. Watch the liquid doesn't boil dry. The water should reduce to a golden-coloured syrup which can be spooned over the whole loin or the ribs when served hot on a bed of steamed rice.

Serves 4

SPICY THAI HAMBURGERS
(LUK NUA)

300 g beef, minced
300 g lean pork, minced
50 g green beans, cut in thin 2 cm slices
2 medium-sized onions, finely chopped
2 cloves garlic, finely chopped
3 tablespoons finely chopped coriander leaves, stems and roots
1 fresh red chilli, finely sliced
1 teaspoon sugar
1 teaspoon pepper
½ teaspoon salt
1 tablespoon red curry paste, bought or homemade (see recipe), optional
1 egg, lightly beaten
½ cup (125 mL) oil, for shallow-frying

In a large bowl combine all ingredients except oil. With wet hands, knead mixture thoroughly until it clings together well. Roll into balls and shape into 5 cm diameter patties, each about 1 cm thick.

Heat oil in wok or frypan and shallow-fry several at a time for 5 minutes or so each side, until evenly browned. Alternatively, grill or barbecue them. Garnish with coriander leaves, if desired.

Serves 4

STEAMED PORK AND VEGETABLE CURRY
(HAW MOK MUU)

This recipe, which is equally delicious with seafood or chicken, is traditionally steamed in a dish made from (or lined with) fresh banana leaves. If you can't find any, line a baking dish with aluminium foil instead.

200 g lean pork, minced or chopped very finely
1 cup (250 mL) coconut milk
2 tablespoons red curry paste, bought or homemade (see recipe)
1 teaspoon dried Kaffir lime leaves, soaked for 10 minutes and finely sliced
2 tablespoons fish sauce
300 g Chinese cabbage, spinach or leeks (any combination)
4 tablespoons thick coconut 'cream', skimmed from top of canned coconut milk before it's shaken
2 tablespoons fresh coriander sprigs

In a large mixing bowl, combine pork, coconut milk, curry paste, lime leaves and fish sauce and mix well. Taste to see if a pinch of sugar, or extra fish sauce is needed, as once you begin steaming you can't stir in more flavours. The sauce should be sweet, spicy and a little salty.

Line a baking dish that will fit inside a steamer with aluminium foil or banana leaves. Then place washed and drained vegetables in the bottom of the dish and cover well with pork and sauce. Garnish with coriander sprigs. Place in steamer and steam for 20 minutes. Garnish with coconut cream spooned over the top, and more coriander leaves.

Serves 4

1. Combine ingredients and mix well.

2. Line a baking dish that will fit inside steamer with banana leaves.

3. Layer ingredients in baking dish starting with vegetables and then pork and sauce.

Steamed Pork and Vegetable Curry is traditionally steamed in banana leaves but aluminium foil does just as well.

BEEF WITH OYSTER SAUCE AND GREENS
(NUA PAD NAMMAN HOI)

200g green vegetables, broccoli,
    spinach, silverbeet, bok choy, beans
    or any combination
2 tablespoons vegetable oil
1 clove garlic, finely sliced
200 g lean beef, cut into thin strips
1 tablespoon oyster sauce
1 tablespoon fish sauce
50 g canned baby corn
50 g champignons, fresh or canned
pinch white pepper
1 teaspoon sugar
3 shallots, chopped

Wash and prepare green vegetables, blanch in a saucepan of boiling water for 1 minute, then drain. Arrange on a serving dish as a bed for the beef.

In a wok or frypan, stir-fry garlic in oil over medium heat until golden. Add beef, stir-fry for several minutes, then add oyster and fish sauces, baby corn, champignons, pepper and sugar. Stir-fry until beef is cooked and tender.

Stir through shallots and cook a further 1 minute. If gravy looks like boiling dry, add a little stock or water with a dash of oyster sauce. Remove from heat and pour over bed of greens. Serve with rice.

Serves 4

BEEF WITH BASIL, CHILLI AND GREEN BEANS
(NUA PAD KRAPAO)

Krapao is one of several varieties of basil grown in Thailand. It's difficult to find outside of Thailand but any locally grown basil will substitute well.

2 tablespoons vegetable oil
1 clove garlic, finely chopped
1 teaspoon fresh chopped chilli
200 g beef, minced or finely chopped
1 teaspoon sugar
1 tablespoon fish sauce
80 g green beans, sliced on an angle
    into 3 cm pieces
1 tablespoon finely sliced onion
5 tablespoons fresh basil leaves
    (reserve a few to garnish)

In a wok or frypan, over medium heat, stir-fry garlic in oil until golden, add chilli and cook for 20 seconds. Add beef and stir-fry for several minutes, stir in sugar and fish sauce and stir-fry until meat is cooked and tender. Add a little water or stock if gravy looks like boiling dry or becoming too oily.

Add beans and onion and taste to see if extra sugar or fish sauce is needed. Remove from heat and stir basil leaves through mixture. Serve with rice and garnish with basil leaves.

Serves 4

MUSLIM BEEF CURRY
(GAENG MUSSAMAN NUA)

3 tablespoons Mussaman curry paste,
    bought or homemade (see recipe)
3 cups (750 mL) coconut milk
100 g fresh pineapple, cut in 2 cm
    cubes (optional)
1 kg lean beef, cut in 2 cm cubes
100 g potatoes, cut in 2 cm cubes
2 tablespoons sugar
1 teaspoon salt
50–100 g roasted peanuts
1 teaspoon tamarind juice
150 g whole pickling onions, or large
    onions quartered with their tops and
    bases intact so they don't break up

In a large saucepan, place the curry paste and 1 cup (250 mL) coconut milk and stir over a low heat. Simmer for a few minutes, then add pineapple pieces and stir for another few minutes. Stir in beef until it's well covered with the sauce, turning frequently.

Add another cup (250 mL) of coconut milk and simmer gently for 15 minutes until meat is chewy, but not tender. Add potatoes and simmer a further 15 minutes until potatoes and meat are tender.

Pour in remaining coconut milk, with sugar, salt, peanuts, tamarind juice and onions and simmer for another 5 minutes until onions are tender. Taste to see if extra tamarind juice, sugar or perhaps some fresh chilli is needed to balance flavours. Serve with rice.

Serves 4

PORK SALAD WITH MINT, PEANUTS AND GINGER
(NAM SOD)

500 g fresh lean pork, minced or finely
    chopped
2 tablespoons water
2 tablespoons lemon juice
2 tablespoons fish sauce
½ teaspoon dried chilli
1 teaspoon finely sliced fresh chilli
2 tablespoons finely sliced onion
2 tablespoons sliced shallots, cut into
    2 cm pieces
2 tablespoons roasted peanuts
2 tablespoons finely sliced fresh
    ginger root
1 tablespoon fresh mint leaves
2 tablespoons chopped fresh coriander
    leaves and stems
6 large lettuce leaves
GARNISH
roasted peanuts, 1 tablespoon finely
    sliced ginger, dried and fresh chilli,
    mint and coriander sprigs, shallot
    curls and chilli flowers (see recipes)

In a large saucepan place minced pork with 2 tablespoons water; cook slowly over medium heat until pork is cooked through but still tender. Remove from heat and add lemon juice, fish sauce, dried and fresh chilli. Stir and when cooled add onion, shallots, peanuts, ginger, mint and coriander leaves. Toss lightly.

Serve on a bed of lettuce leaves and garnish with mounds of peanuts, ginger and chilli. Decorate with sprigs of mint and coriander, shallot curls and chilli flowers.

Serves 4

MEATY SALADS
Thai cuisine blurs the line between main meat dishes and salads. Many Thai salads and vegetable side dishes use meat or fish. Contrasting colours and textures are as important as nutritional balance.

Pork Salad with Mint, Peanuts and Ginger. Here we've chopped the pork but the Thais usually mince the meat very finely for this recipe.

SPICY BEEF CURRY
(GAENG PA NUA)

3 cups (750 mL) beef or chicken Thai
Soup Stock (see recipe)
4 tablespoons red curry paste, bought
or homemade (see recipe)
2 pieces galangal, soaked 5 minutes
and sliced
1 tablespoon dried krachai, soaked ½
hour in warm water, then finely cut
(optional — see Note)
1 teaspoon ground cumin
1 teaspoon ground coriander
1 tablespoon dried Kaffir lime leaves
1 tablespoon fish sauce
500 g lean beef, sliced
pinch sugar or sliced fresh chilli
(optional)
50 g eggplant pieces or bamboo
shoots, green beans, zucchini or
fresh asparagus
2 tablespoons fresh basil leaves
fresh coriander leaves, to garnish

In a saucepan, bring ½ cup (125 mL)
stock to the boil, then add curry paste,
galangal, krachai, cumin, coriander and
lime leaves. Stir rapidly to combine
ingredients thoroughly and release the
flavours. Add remaining stock, again
bring to the boil, then add fish sauce and
beef and simmer until tender.

Taste to see if extra fish sauce, or perhaps a pinch or two of sugar, is needed
to balance the flavours. If you prefer the
curry a little spicier, add some sliced
fresh chilli.

Add the eggplant a few minutes before
serving, remove from heat and stir in the
basil leaves. Garnish with coriander
leaves and serve with rice.

Serves 4

Note: Krachai, also known as 'lesser ginger' is available dried in packets at Asian
foodstores. It has a mild flavour and the
recipe will not suffer too much if you
delete it.

ROAST OR BARBECUED PORK WITH SPICY DIPPING SAUCE
(JITTRA MUU YAHNG)

400 g lean pork, fillets or steaks
MARINADE
2 tablespoons vegetable oil
1 teaspoon sugar
1 teaspoon fish sauce
SAUCE
1 tablespoon vegetable oil
2 large fresh tomatoes, halved, grilled
and neatly diced
1 tablespoon finely chopped lemon
grass
1 tablespoon chopped coriander root
1 tablespoon dried galangal pieces,
soaked for 5 minutes in hot water
and sliced
1 tablespoon chopped onion
1 tablespoon chopped garlic
½ cup (125 mL) chicken Thai Soup
Stock (see recipe)
3 tablespoons fish sauce
3 tablespoons sugar
1 teaspoon chilli powder
2 tablespoons tamarind juice
1 tablespoon chopped fresh coriander
leaves
GARNISH
1 large green cucumber, sliced and
fresh coriander sprigs

Combine marinade ingredients, rub over
pork and marinate for at least 2 hours.
Roast, barbecue or grill pork for 10 minutes on each side or until cooked
through. Set aside.

To make sauce, in a saucepan, saute
in oil half the diced tomato and all the
lemon grass, coriander root, galangal,
onion and garlic for about 5 minutes.
Place in a food processor with chicken
stock and blend until smooth.

Remove and return sauce to saucepan
and stir over a medium heat. Then add
fish sauce, sugar, chilli powder, tamarind
juice and cook for another few minutes.
Taste to see if extra sugar, fish sauce or
tamarind juice is required.

Remove from heat and pour into serving bowl. Stir in remaining diced tomato
and chopped coriander leaves.

Before serving, slice pork thinly and
arrange in several rows on a large platter
surrounded by sliced cucumber. Garnish
with coriander sprigs. Serve with sauce
and steamed rice.

Serves 4

1. Marinate pork for at least 2 hours.

*Roast or Barbecued Pork with Spicy
Dipping Sauce. Cook the pork to your
own liking then dip and eat.*

2. Pork can be roasted, grilled or barbecued.

3. Make sauce in a pan then blend until smooth.

4. Reheat and add remaining ingredients.

CUTTING, CHOPPING AND CARVING

Thai cooks are famous for their skilful fruit and vegetable carving, but their everyday dexterity with the cleaver shouldn't be underestimated either.

They place a great deal of importance on just how meat and vegetables are cut. It often depends on the type of dish and the quality of the ingredients. Basically, most ingredients in a particular dish are cut similarly, whether sliced, diced or chopped. It's not a hard and fast rule (as in most of Thai cooking, use discretion), yet there are subtle changes in flavour depending on the way the ingredients are cut.

SLICING

When slicing meat, cut on the diagonal, slicing across the fibres or grain. The same applies to tough, stringy or round vegetables. Softer or long vegetables are more often sliced along or parallel to the fibres, e.g. beans, mushrooms or shallots.

DICING

When dicing, or cutting into small pieces, uniformity of size is important, and cubes should be bite-sized in general. The Thais often say bite-sized is the amount which fits on a spoon half-filled with rice. But that depends on the size of the spoon! Cubes from 1—4 cm, depending on the texture of the ingredient, will do.

CHOPPING

Chopping is something the Thais do with two sharp knives or cleavers, with the end result often as fine as minced meat. Their dexterity with two knives at once is awesome. Unless you have years to practise, it's safer to use a food processor or mincer to get the desired effect. When you want minced pork ask your butcher to do it for you, though they usually like a day's notice.

You will find several large sharp knives and at least one large cleaver are invaluable when you become serious about Thai cooking. Observing a Thai chef in action with a cleaver is really something. He'll cut up a whole chicken, bones and all, in seconds, slice and dice some vegetables, then grab another cleaver and with one in each hand, reduce a lump of pork to mincemeat. He'll then tilt the cleaver on its side and deftly carry the ingredients on its wide blade to the waiting wok.

Some Thai cooking utensils — all useful but not essential. As long as you have sharp knives, a chopping board, a steamer and several sturdy saucepans you can get started. A wok, cleaver and some stirring implements are certainly handy.

Credit: Appley Hoare Antiques; Made in Japan Imports; Good Luck Grocery Store

CARVING

Thais are renowned for their fruit and vegetable carving. Humble tomatoes, cucumbers, radishes and watermelons become objets d'art in the hands of a Thai housewife. It's a skill that takes years to learn, but here are some of the less difficult decorative methods for you to experiment with.

TOMATO BASKETS
1. Cut the top neatly off a firm red smooth tomato.
2. Cut two even pieces away with two vertical and two horizontal slices, forming the exterior of a basket. Make zigzag edges, if you can.
3. Scoop out the pulp and seeds, leaving a basket.

SHALLOT CURLS
1. Take any part of the shallot stem or bulk and cut into a 6 cm piece.
2. Keeping a base of about 1 cm intact, slice stem several times lengthways.
3. Place in iced water for ends to curl back.

CHILLI FLOWER
1. Holding the stem with your finger, place chilli on cutting board, then slit chilli several times lengthways, cutting from the base to the point.
2. The cuts can be made spiky to give jagged edges.
3. Place into iced water and petals will curl out. Usually the more cuts and the finer they are, the more the petals will curl. Remove seeds after the flowers have opened.

WATERMELONS, SMOOTH-SKINNED PUMPKINS AND GOURDS
1. Cut off top and stem and discard. Hollow out, reserving flesh but discarding seeds. Leave hull 5 cm thick.
2. Cut around rim continuous V shapes of equal size.
3. Repeat in layers until you have decorated the melon. The skin colour can be used to contrast with the colour of the underlayer.
4. Invert before serving, chill and fill with fruit salads, soups, fried rice or sauces.

CUCUMBER LEAF

1. Thickly peel off slices of cucumber lengthways and cut into rectangles about 6 cm by 3 cm.
2. Cut a leaf shape out of each piece, then cut the perimeter into rib-like notches.
3. Gouge out a thin strip along the middle to make a main rib. Then cut smaller ribs spreading out to sides. Place in a bowl of iced water until ready to use.

RADISH AND TURNIP FLOWERS

1. Using a small sharp knife, make a series of regular slits around the vegetable, from the tip almost to the bottom, leaving the base of 1 cm intact.
2. Place it in iced water for the outer 'petals' to open out.
3. Remove from water and repeat a second circle of slits. Place in water, then repeat, until tip of vegetable is reduced to a thin stick. This can be quartered lengthways.
4. Place in iced water until needed.

CUCUMBER LOTUS

1. Cut ends off a small cucumber and divide it in two. Do not peel.
2. Mark, with a knife, eight equal triangles on the top surface of each piece. Then continue each triangle down the length of the cucumber pieces. Cut along the lines through to the centre, but don't cut through to the base, keeping everything joined at the bottom.
3. Shape the top of each triangle to make an arch or petal.
4. Cut the outline of each petal around the skin surface, inserting the knife as far as you can into the centre of the cucumber.
5. Cut in a circle about 4 mm from the edge down to about 4 mm from the bottom, still keeping the base attached. Repeat again another 4 mm in from the last circle, and again if the cucumber is wide enough. Scoop out any soft flesh in the middle.
6. Place pieces in iced water for 10 minutes for the petals to open. Put tomato roses in their centres and trim with herbs.

TOMATO ROSE

1. Cut the top neatly off a firm red tomato. Reserve the top.
2. Finely slice across the tomato, from the same end, a slice which is still attached to the skin and in a spiral motion continue peeling the tomato in one continuous strip.
3. Roll the tomato strip into a rose shape with the sliced top forming a base.

FISH, PRAWNS AND OTHER SEAFOOD DISHES

With a vast coastline and thousands of kilometres of wide rivers and streams, it's no wonder the Thais' chief source of protein is fish and seafood.

There's an abundance of freshwater and saltwater fish, and plenty of fresh crabs, prawns, mussels, lobsters and calamari.

Elsewhere, stiff packets of dried and salted fish can be bought in Asian foodstores. To eat them, you deep-fry them in vegetable oil and serve as a side dish to counter spicy curries.

When recipes call for fresh whole fish or fillets, use firm, white-fleshed fish such as snapper, bream, cod, haddock or whiting.

STIR-FRIED SEAFOOD WITH FRESH HERBS
(AHAHN TALAY)

This is a dish to feature at a Thai banquet. We've suggested one seafood combination but it's up to you. See what seafood is the freshest and best value on the day, and create your own combination.

100 g fish fillets
6 mussels
1 small cooked crab
100 g calamari pieces
100 g green (uncooked) prawns
100 g scallops
2 cloves garlic, chopped
2 large fresh chillies, chopped
1 tablespoon chopped coriander root
3 tablespoons vegetable oil
2 tablespoons oyster sauce
2 tablespoons fish sauce
1 capsicum, cut in strips
1 onion, sliced
2 shallots, cut in 2 cm slices
4 tablespoons fresh basil, mint or
    oregano leaves
additional fresh herbs of your choice,
    to garnish

Wash and prepare seafood, cutting fillets into smaller pieces. Scrub the mussels, removing beards. Take limbs off crab and crack shells so the meat is easy to remove at the table. Remove outer shell, clean out crab body, and break into edible pieces. Put seafood aside.

Make a rough paste out of garlic, chillies and coriander root either with a mortar and pestle or processor. Put aside. Arrange all the ingredients so you're ready to start cooking.

Heat oil in a wok and fry the garlic, chilli, and coriander root paste over medium heat until flavours are released. Add seafood and stir-fry gently so the softer fish pieces don't break up.

Add oyster sauce and fish sauce, then taste to see whether more fish sauce or water is required to balance spicy flavours. Cover with a lid and simmer for a few minutes if seafood needs more cooking. Add capsicum, onion, shallots and fresh herbs, stir-fry for 2 minutes, then remove from heat.

Arrange on a large shallow serving platter or bowl and garnish with your choice of fresh herbs. Serve with steaming rice.

Serves 4

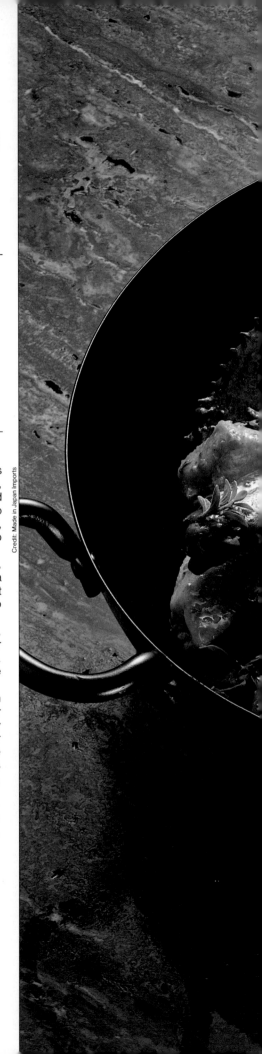

Stir-fried Seafood with Fresh Herbs. Create your own combination with the best value catches of the day.

Credit: Made in Japan Imports

WHOLE FISH WITH GINGER SAUCE
(PLA JIAN)

700 g whole fish (snapper or bream)
1 tablespoon vegetable oil
1 clove garlic, finely chopped
2 shallots, cut in 2 cm pieces
1 tablespoon finely chopped ginger root
1 teaspoon chopped pickled soy bean or 1 tablespoon fish sauce
1½ tablespoons sugar
1 tablespoon ground turmeric
1 cup (250 mL) chicken stock or water
1 tablespoon tamarind juice
½ teaspoon white pepper
1 tablespoon cornflour mixed to a thin paste with cold water
1 tablespoon sliced capsicum, cut into fine strips
2 tablespoons sliced onion
2 tablespoons dried wood fungus, soaked in warm water for 10 minutes (optional)
6 sprigs fresh coriander, for garnish

Wash and trim fish, pat dry, then grill, fry or steam whole. (If grilling, place on greased aluminium foil.) Put fish aside and keep warm.

Heat oil in a wok or saucepan over medium heat and add garlic, shallots, ginger, pickled soy bean if using, and sugar. Stir, reduce heat and cook for several minutes until flavours blend well.

Add turmeric, stock, tamarind juice and pepper (and fish sauce if using instead of pickled soy bean) then taste for balanced flavour. The sauce should be sweet, slightly salty, with a hint of sourness.

Remove from heat and stir in several teaspoons of the cornflour paste, then return to a low heat. Add a little more, if necessary, stirring, until the sauce is smooth. Stir in capsicum, onion and wood fungus and stir once or twice. Remove from heat.

Using tongs, place fish on a platter, pour sauce over fish from head to tail. Garnish with coriander sprigs and serve with rice.

Serves 4

1. *Wash and trim fish then pat dry before cooking.*

2. *Make sauce in a wok or saucepan, cooking for several minutes so that the flavours blend well.*

3. *Pour sauce over fish in one movement from head to tail.*

Whole Fish with Ginger Sauce is so simple. Just grill, fry or steam the fish then cover with the easy-to-make sauce, and garnish.

CHILLI PRAWNS
(GOONG PAD PRIK)

2 tablespoons vegetable oil
1 clove garlic, chopped
1 tablespoon sliced fresh chilli
200 g large, green (uncooked) prawns,
    peeled, deveined, and tails intact
3 tablespoons water
1 tablespoon fish sauce
1 tablespoon oyster sauce
1 onion, sliced
2 shallots, cut into 2 cm pieces

Heat oil in a wok or large frypan over
medium heat and stir-fry garlic until
golden. Add chilli and prawns, stir-fry to
absorb flavours for 2 minutes, then add
water. Simmer until prawns are pink and
just cooked. Add fish and oyster sauces,
onion and shallots, stir several times and
serve.

Serves 4

STIR-FRIED MUSSELS WITH CHILLI, GARLIC AND BASIL
(PAD HOI MANG PU)

3 fresh chillies, chopped
2 cloves garlic, chopped
1 tablespoon chopped coriander root
3 tablespoons vegetable oil
2 tablespoons oyster sauce
1 tablespoon fish sauce
500 g mussels, scrubbed, beards
    removed
½ cup (125 mL) chicken Thai Soup
    Stock (see recipe) or water
4 tablespoons chopped fresh basil or
    coriander leaves

Pound chillies, garlic and coriander root
in mortar or process to a rough paste in
processor. Stir-fry paste with oil in wok or
frypan over medium heat until flavours
blend well. Add oyster and fish sauces,
stir, add mussels and stock. Cover and
simmer for 10 minutes until mussels
open and are cooked. Taste to see if
extra fish sauce or water is needed to
balance flavours.

Stir in some basil and remove from
heat. Arrange mussels on a platter or
shallow bowl, pour sauce over them and
serve with rice or a salad.

Serves 4

*Stir-fried Mussels with Chilli, Garlic and
Basil.*

PRAWNS
*Prawns, also known as shrimps,
are very much a part of the Thai
diet. Our recipes usually specify
whether to use large or small,
cooked or uncooked prawns.
Those recipes which do not
specify, are flexible: it is up to the
cook to use whatever she or he
has available or finds convenient.*

*Prawnmeat is also available
frozen in supermarkets, and may
sometimes be substituted in the
recipes.*

STUFFED, STEAMED WHOLE CRABS
(POO CHA)

5 cooked blue swimmer crabs
FILLING
200 g lean pork, chopped
1 onion, chopped
1 teaspoon pepper
1 tablespoon sugar
1 tablespoon fish sauce
1 tablespoon chopped coriander root
2 eggs, separated
1 tablespoon chopped shallots
**1 tablespoon chopped fresh coriander
    leaves**
2 fresh chillies, finely sliced

Remove limbs from crabs. Clean out body shells, keeping them intact so they can be filled. Remove all meat from the limbs and body, and reserve.

To make filling, in a food processor combine pork, onion, pepper, sugar, fish sauce and coriander root. Remove from processor and place in a bowl with the flaked crab meat and one egg white. Add shallots and chopped coriander leaves and mix by hand, using some more egg white if necessary to hold together well.

Fill each crab shell making a mound to follow the shape of the shell. Carefully break the surface of an egg yolk; taking about ½ teaspoon of yolk, place a dollop on the top of each mound of crab filling, then sprinkle with sliced chilli. Take care not to move the crabs suddenly or the yolk dollops will run.

If you find the garnish exercise a little difficult, brush the filling instead with beaten egg yolk and sprinkle with sliced chilli and some coriander leaves.

Place each crab, stuffed side up, in a large steamer and steam for 20 minutes. Serve with a Thai salad or fresh greens. Garnish with chilli flowers and shallot curls (see recipes).

Serves 4

VARIATION:

STUFFED, STEAMED WHOLE LOBSTER
(GOONG TALAY CHA)

Use one large cooked lobster instead of crab. Clean out head, body and tail, reserving all edible meat. Be careful not to damage the lobster and leave limbs and head intact. Fill the head, body and tail with same filling mixture as for recipe above, using lobster meat instead of crab meat, and brush with beaten egg yolk.

Steam, then serve so filling is hidden under lobster, and it sits up lifelike on a serving plate decorated with garnishes of your choice.

1. *Remove limbs from crabs. Clean shells keeping them intact so they can be filled.*

2. Make filling by combining ingredients in food processor.

3. Fill each shell, making a mound to follow the shape of the shell.

4. Dollop egg yolk on top of each mound and sprinkle with chilli. Take care moving the crabs or the egg yolk will run.

5. Place in steamer and cook for 20 minutes.

SALTED FISH
(PLA KEM)

Salting and drying fish was a way of preserving it in a country with little refrigeration outside the cities. Salted foods also have their own, sometimes acquired, appeal. Thais living outside Thailand now pay dearly for that acquired taste, because the dried and salted fish available in overseas Chinatowns and Asian foodstores is not cheap.

Salted Fish is fried and eaten as an accompaniment to spicy dishes. The saltiness is a balance to the heat of chillies. The recipe below is for salted fresh fish — less expensive to eat here, but with the same soothing effect on the palate when eating curries.

4 × 200 g whole fish, cleaned, trimmed with heads intact
3 tablespoons coarse salt
vegetable oil, for deep-frying
fresh coriander leaves and cucumber slices to garnish

Score both sides of fish then rub well with salt. Stack fish in layers in a covered bowl and marinate at least overnight or preferably for 24 hours.

Deep-fry whole fish until golden. Garnish with coriander leaves and cucumber slices, and serve with curries.

Serves 4

WHOLE FISH WITH FRESH CHILLI, GARLIC AND CORIANDER
(PLA LAD PRIK)

3 large fresh chillies, roughly chopped
1 coriander root, chopped
2 cloves garlic, roughly chopped
700 g whole fish (snapper or bream)
1 tablespoon vegetable oil
1½ tablespoons sugar
1½ tablespoons fish sauce
½ cup (125 mL) chicken Thai Soup Stock (see recipe) or water
1 tablespoon lemon juice
1 tablespoon cornflour mixed to a thin paste with cold water
GARNISH
1 tablespoon chopped fresh coriander leaves
2 fresh red chillies or capsicum, cut in fine strips
6 sprigs fresh coriander

Pound together or process chillies, coriander root and garlic to make a paste and put aside. Wash, trim, dry and score fish, and cook: grill on greased aluminium foil, steam or fry. Put fish aside and keep warm.

Heat oil over medium heat in a saucepan and stir-fry spice paste, sugar and fish sauce until sugar dissolves and flavours blend well. Pour in stock, stir and simmer for a few minutes. Stir in lemon juice, taste, and if necessary add some more sugar, fish sauce or lemon juice to balance flavours. Check liquid level before thickening sauce. If there is not enough liquid, add a little more water or stock, stir, then remove from heat.

Add cornflour paste a teaspoon at a time, and stir. Don't make the sauce too thick — it should be clear and slightly runny. Return to medium heat for a few stirs, then remove from stove.

Place fish on a large platter and pour sauce over it from head to tail. Sprinkle with chopped coriander leaves and garnish with chilli or capsicum strips and coriander sprigs. Serve with steamed rice.

Serves 4

Salted Fish

SCALLOPS WITH CHILLI AND BASIL
(PAD PRIK HOI)

250 g fresh scallops
4 tablespoons red curry paste, bought
**   or homemade (see recipe)**
2 tablespoons vegetable oil
2 cloves garlic, finely chopped
2 fresh red chillies, finely sliced
2 tablespoons fish sauce
1 tablespoon sugar
6 tablespoons fresh basil leaves

Combine scallops with curry paste and marinate for 15 minutes. In a wok or large frypan, heat vegetable oil and stir-fry garlic until golden. Add marinated scallops, curry paste and chillies, and stir-fry for 2 minutes. Add fish sauce and sugar, stir and cook another minute, then taste. If needed, add extra fish sauce, sugar or chilli.

When scallops are cooked and tender, stir through most of the basil leaves, then remove from heat. Garnish with remaining basil leaves and serve with rice.

Serves 4

PRAWNS WITH GARLIC AND PEPPER SERVED WITH GREENS
(GOONG TOD GRATEUM)

500 g green (uncooked) king prawns
1 medium-sized leek or 50 g chopped
**   zucchini or spinach**
4 tablespoons vegetable oil
1 tablespoon finely chopped garlic
1 teaspoon white pepper
1 teaspoon sugar
1 tablespoon fish sauce
fresh coriander sprigs, to garnish

Peel and devein prawns, discarding heads but leaving tails intact. Flatten slightly with the back of a spoon into a butterfly shape.

Halve leek vertically and soak in water to clean. Cut into 2.5 cm pieces and blanch for 1 minute in boiling water. Drain, then place neatly to form a bed on a serving plate.

Lightly stir-fry prawns in oil in a wok or frypan. Turn them over and add garlic, pepper, sugar and fish sauce. Briefly stir-fry, avoiding overcooking. Pour prawns and sauce over leek pieces and garnish with coriander. Serve with rice.

Serves 4

Scallops with Chilli and Basil. Take care not to overcook them.

CHILLI CRAB
(POO PAD PRIK)

1 kg cooked crabs
3 large fresh chillies, chopped
2 cloves garlic, chopped
1 tablespoon chopped coriander root
3 tablespoons cooking oil
1 cup (250 mL) water
2 tablespoons oyster sauce
2 tablespoons fish sauce
3 shallots, cut into 2 cm pieces
1 onion, sliced
5–6 tablespoons whole fresh coriander
**   leaves, (reserving a few for garnish)**

Clean crabs and break into pieces, cracking shells on legs and claws so they're easy to pull apart at the table. Put crab pieces aside and arrange ingredients ready to cook.

Make a rough paste out of the chillies, garlic and coriander root, either in a mortar with a pestle, or by briefly processing. Heat oil in a large frypan or wok. Stir-fry paste for several minutes to allow flavours to be released. Add crab pieces and briefly stir-fry, smearing well with the paste. Add 1 cup (250 mL) water and bring mixture to the boil. Reduce heat, cover and simmer for 20 minutes.

Remove lid and add oyster and fish sauces. Stir and taste. If necessary, add more fish sauce or water to balance spicy and salty flavours.

Stir in shallots, onion and coriander leaves, and cook for another minute. Remove from heat and serve in a large shallow bowl. Garnish with coriander leaves and serve with rice or salad.

Serves 4

Credit: Lifestyle Imports, Dansab

STEAMED MUSSELS WITH LIME LEAVES AND GALANGAL
(HOI MANG PU OB MORDIN)

2 tablespoons lemon grass, sliced into
   2 cm pieces
2 pieces galangal
5 dried Kaffir lime leaves
500 g mussels, scrubbed, beards
   removed

In a large saucepan, boil 2 cups (500 mL) water and add lemon grass, galangal and lime leaves and cook for 2 minutes. Add mussels, cover saucepan with lid, and cook for 15 minutes until mussels open. Stir occasionally.

Warm a serving tureen or deep casserole and when mussels are ready, take out galangal and lime leaves and place in bottom of dish. Arrange mussels on top of them, and pour liquid over all. Serve with Spicy Seafood Sauce (see recipe). Dip and eat!

Serves 4

SWEET AND SOUR PRAWNS
(PAD PREOW WAN GOONG)

2 tablespoons vegetable oil
1 clove garlic, chopped
50 g pineapple, diced
1 tomato, diced
½ cucumber, diced
1 teaspoon lemon juice
1 tablespoon sugar
1½ tablespoons fish sauce
1 tablespoon oyster sauce
2 tablespoons bottled tomato sauce
3 tablespoons chicken Thai Soup Stock
   (see recipe) or water
200 g large raw prawns, deveined,
   shelled but with tails intact
2 shallots, cut into 2 cm pieces
1 onion, sliced

Heat oil in wok and stir-fry garlic until golden. Add pineapple, tomato, cucumber, lemon juice, sugar, fish, oyster and tomato sauces. Stir until mixture turns golden.

Pour in stock, simmer for 1 minute, stir, then add prawns. Cook prawns until they're pink and tender, adding a little more water if necessary. Taste to see if more lemon juice, sugar or fish sauce is required to balance flavours.

Just before serving, stir in shallots and onion and cook for 1 minute. Serve with rice.

Serves 4

STIR-FRIED STUFFED CALAMARI
(PLA MEUK SOD SAI)

500 g calamari tubes
150 g sliced leeks, choko or spinach
5 tablespoons vegetable oil
1 tablespoon finely chopped garlic
1 teaspoon white pepper
1 tablespoon fish sauce
1½ tablespoons oyster sauce
fresh coriander, mint or basil leaves, to
   garnish
FILLING
300 g pork, minced
2 tablespoons sliced onion
2 coriander roots, finely chopped
½ tablespoon white pepper
½ tablespoon sugar
1 teaspoon fish sauce

Place all filling ingredients in a food processor and mince finely. Fill calamari tubes to three-quarters full with stuffing, close and secure with toothpicks at both ends. Put aside ready to cook. Prepare vegetables and blanch for 1 minute in boiling water. Drain thoroughly and arrange on a serving dish as a bed for the calamari.

In a large frypan or wok, gently stir-fry stuffed calamari in 3 tablespoons vegetable oil for about 5 minutes. Turn them carefully now and then, but be careful not to break them. Don't try to brown them. Remove and put aside.

In the same frypan, stir-fry garlic, pepper, fish and oyster sauces, then return stuffed calamari to pan. Adding extra oil as necessary, stir-fry several minutes, occasionally turning them over. Remove from heat and arrange calamari on the bed of greens. Cover with sauce and garnish with fresh coriander, mint or basil leaves.

Serves 4

SPICY MUSSELS WITH CHILLI AND LIME LEAVES
(GAENG CHOO CHEE HOI MANG PU)

500 g mussels, scrubbed, beards
   removed
4 dried Kaffir lime leaves
2 pieces galangal
1 stem lemon grass, chopped into 2 cm
   pieces
1 cup (250 mL) coconut milk
2 tablespoons red or green curry paste,
   bought or homemade (see recipe)
1 teaspoon sugar
1 tablespoon fish sauce (optional)
GARNISH
fresh basil leaves, mint leaves, chilli or
   capsicum strips

In a large saucepan place 3 cups (750 mL) water and boil mussels, lime leaves, galangal and lemon grass, until mussels just open, about 5 minutes. Strain and reserve mussels, lime leaves, galangal and lemon grass. Also reserve stock in case a little is needed for the sauce.

In a saucepan or wok, heat coconut milk and bring to the boil. Add curry paste and sugar, and simmer for several minutes. Add reserved lime leaves, galangal and lemon grass and simmer for another few minutes. Then add mussels, stirring sauce through them to absorb flavours. Taste to see if fish sauce is required (it may be salty enough) and if extra sugar or water is needed to balance flavours.

Remove from heat and arrange mussels on a serving bowl or dish. Pour sauce over mussels and decorate with garnishes of your choice. Serve with rice or a salad.

Serves 4

SPICY SEAFOOD SAUCE
(NAM PRIK GUER)

2 cloves garlic, roughly chopped
2 tablespoons chopped fresh chilli
3 tablespoons lemon juice
2 tablespoons vinegar
1 teaspoon sugar
1 teaspoon salt
1 tablespoon fish sauce
2 coriander roots, chopped
chopped fresh coriander leaves, to
   serve

Blend all sauce ingredients in a food processor, then taste to see if more fish sauce, lemon juice, vinegar or sugar is required. Add some boiled water if necessary to get the consistency you like. Garnish with chopped coriander leaves stirred in just before serving.

Makes 1 cup (250 mL)

CALAMARI AND MUSSELS

Calamari is also known as squid. Recipes specify which part of the squid to buy. In general, choose the tubes (the main part of the body, with head and tentacles removed) prepared by your local fish market. These save you a lot of work and are more tender than the prepared calamari rings.

Mussels can be replaced by cockles or winkles.

STIR-FRIED CALAMARI WITH PEPPER AND GARLIC
(PLA MEUK TOD GRATEUM)

This dish includes some green vegetables as a bed for the calamari pieces. It's important to use fresh, tender calamari. Buy whole tubes (not whole squid, which is a lot of work) instead of ready-cut calamari rings, (which are often the offcuts and too tough). As a rule, tubes that are thick and spongy are more tender than the thinner ones. A visit to the local fish market is worth the trouble to get really fresh, good quality seafood. Smaller fish shops may not have the range.

200 g calamari tubes
150 g sliced leeks, zucchini or choko, cut into 3 cm pieces
2 tablespoons vegetable oil
½ tablespoon finely chopped garlic
1 teaspoon oyster sauce
½ teaspoon white pepper
½ teaspoon sugar
1 tablespoon fish sauce
chopped fresh coriander, to garnish (optional)

Cut through calamari tubes, score in cross hatch pattern, then cut into 3 cm squares. Blanch green vegetables in boiling water, drain and place in a mound on a serving platter.

Heat oil in wok or large frypan over medium heat, and add calamari pieces, garlic, oyster sauce, pepper and sugar, then stir slowly until calamari is cooked and tender. This depends on the calamari, but is usually 5–10 minutes. Add fish sauce, stir, then taste to see if more oyster sauce, sugar or fish sauce is needed to balance salty and sweet flavours.

Arrange calamari over the bed of greens and pour sauce over them. Garnish with chopped coriander if desired, and serve with rice.

Serves 4

Stir-fried Calamari with Pepper and Garlic served on a bed of blanched leeks, and Sweet and Sour Prawns.

SPICY HOT SAUCE WITH FRESH PRAWN PIECES
(NAM PRIK GOONG SOD)

The rich sauce in this recipe goes well with noodles, rice or pasta. It's also served with steamed cauliflower, broccoli pieces, cabbage or spinach. Pour the sauce over a bowl of steamed leafy vegetables and rice, and serve.

1 tablespoon oil
100 g fresh red and green chillies, or less if preferred
1 onion, chopped
4 tablespoons chopped garlic
1 tablespoon chopped coriander root
1½ tablespoons shrimp paste
1 cup (250 mL) water
200 g large green (uncooked) prawns
2 tablespoons fish sauce
2 tablespoons lemon juice
2 tablespoons chopped fresh coriander leaves
2 tablespoons finely chopped shallots

Over medium heat in a wok or frypan, saute chillies briefly in oil, remove and set aside on a plate. Saute onion, garlic and coriander root until onion is golden and clear. Remove and put aside with chillies. Wrap shrimp paste in aluminium foil and dry-fry each side for several minutes. Put aside on the plate.

In a saucepan bring water to the boil and add prawns with the shells on. Boil for several minutes then remove, reserving prawn stock. Peel prawns, cut into bite-sized pieces and set aside.

In a food processor combine cooked chillies, onion, garlic, coriander, shrimp paste and half the prawn stock. Process into a sauce using extra stock if necessary, but be careful not to make it too thin or mushy. Pour into a bowl and stir in fish sauce, lemon juice and prawn pieces. Just before serving, stir in coriander leaves and shallots. The sauce will keep in the refrigerator for two days.

Serves 4

LOBSTERS AND CRABS
Recipes specify whether to buy cooked or uncooked lobsters and crabs. If lobsters are unavailable, substitute crayfish. If blue swimmer crabs are unavailable, use any edible crabs recommended by your local fish market.

Whole Fish in Red Curry Sauce with Lime Leaves and Seafood Omelette. Both can be made with a minimum of fuss.

WHOLE FISH IN RED CURRY SAUCE WITH LIME LEAVES
(GAENG PLA CHOO CHEE)

A quick curry dish equally stunning with large green (uncooked) prawns or lobster tails. It's a fine centrepiece for a Thai feast, but, with some red curry paste on hand, is simple to make.

650 g whole bream or similar fish
1 cup (250 mL) vegetable oil (reserve 1 tablespoon for stir-frying curry paste)
1½ teaspoons red curry paste, bought or homemade (see recipe)
1 fresh red chilli, seeded, finely sliced
6 dried Kaffir lime leaves
1 cup (250 mL) coconut milk
1 tablespoon fish sauce
1 teaspoon sugar
GARNISH
fresh coriander, basil or young citrus leaves
lemon wedges
capsicum or chilli, cut in strips
sliced cucumber and tomato

Wash, pat dry then trim fish by cutting off sharp spikes. Score both sides with a fork. In a wok or large frypan over high heat, cook fish using most of the vegetable oil, until golden on one side. Lower heat and using two tongs gently turn fish over. Turn up heat again to cook until golden. It will take about 5 minutes each side. Using tongs again, lift fish gently onto a serving plate.

In the wok, gently stir-fry red curry paste, red chilli and lime leaves in remaining tablespoon of oil. Add coconut milk, fish sauce and sugar and simmer for about 5 minutes. Taste to see if extra coconut milk, fish sauce or sugar is required.

Pour sauce over fish and garnish with fresh leaves, lemon wedges, fine strips of capsicum or chilli and sliced cucumber and tomato. Serve with rice.

Serves 4

MINCED FISH AND EGGPLANT CURRY
(GAENG SUP NOK PLA)

2 tablespoons vegetable oil
2 tablespoons red or green curry paste, bought or homemade (see recipe)
1 tablespoon dried Kaffir lime leaves, soaked for 10 minutes and sliced
2 cups (500 mL) coconut milk
500 g fish fillets, minced (ocean perch, redfish, etc)
2 tablespoons fish sauce
1 eggplant or 2 zucchini, diced
1 tablespoon whole basil leaves

In a wok or large saucepan, stir-fry curry paste and lime leaves in oil then add ½ cup (125 mL) coconut milk and simmer until the oil rises and liquid turns green.

Add minced fish and stir slowly until fish is well separated, then add remaining coconut milk. Stir in fish sauce and eggplant and simmer for another 5–10 minutes, until sauce is required consistency.

Remove from heat and stir in basil leaves. Serve as a spicy sauce over noodles, spaghetti or rice.

Serves 4

SEAFOOD OMELETTE
(KAI YAD SAI AHAHN TALAY)

2 cloves garlic, chopped
1 small onion, chopped
2 tablespoons chopped fresh coriander root
2 tablespoons vegetable oil
150 g chopped fresh seafood e.g. green (uncooked) prawns, scallops, crabmeat or calamari
½ tablespoon fish sauce
1 teaspoon sugar
1 teaspoon black pepper
3 tablespoons chopped fresh coriander leaves
4 eggs, lightly beaten with 1 tablespoon fish sauce

In a mortar, pound garlic, onion and coriander root to a paste. Then stir-fry paste in half the vegetable oil, in a wok or frypan, for about 1 minute. Add chopped seafood and stir-fry until cooked. Season with fish sauce, sugar and pepper, taste for flavour, then stir through half the coriander leaves. Put aside.

In an omelette pan or frypan, heat remaining tablespoon of oil over medium heat, then pour in the egg and fish sauce mixture. When omelette begins to set, put seafood mixture in the centre and fold sides of omelette over to form a square. When omelette is golden underneath, turn it over like a pancake and brown the other side.

Serve as a whole omelette or sliced. If smaller omelettes are required adjust proportions and/or cook in smaller quantities. Garnish with the remaining chopped coriander leaves.

Serves 4

CHICKEN, AND OTHER POULTRY DISHES

Chicken features predominantly in Thai cuisine. Its mild flavour combines well with fresh herbs, vegetables or spicy curries.

Poultry can be boned and served as bite-sized pieces in stir-fried dishes, curries, satays and salads; or it can be served in larger pieces, keeping the bones, in casseroles and roasts.

Credit: Made in Japan Imports; Appley Hoare Antiques

DUCK CASSEROLE
(TOM KEM PED)

3 cloves garlic
3 large coriander roots
10 peppercorns, cracked
4 tablespoons sugar
1.5 kg fresh young duck, whole or in pieces
1 tablespoon soy sauce
1 teaspoon salt
100 g dried Chinese mushrooms, soaked in water 30 minutes, stems discarded
2.5 cm piece fresh ginger root
4–6 eggs, hard-boiled and peeled
6 carrot pieces, about 5 cm each

With a mortar and pestle or food processor, make a rough paste from garlic, coriander roots and peppercorns. Set aside.

In a large saucepan, heat sugar and 1 tablespoon water until it caramelises into a dark brown syrup. Be careful not to let it burn. Remove pan from heat and stir in ½ cup (125 mL) water. Place duck in the saucepan and return to medium heat. Coat duck in liquid and brown all over, stirring occasionally. Add soy sauce, salt and spice paste and more water to cover the duck, if necessary. Bring to the boil, add mushrooms and ginger, reduce heat and simmer gently for about 25 minutes. Add eggs and carrots and simmer for a further 20 minutes or until duck is tender.

Spoon into serving dish. Halve the eggs, and arrange with carrots and mushrooms on top of duck. Serve accompanied by a platter of cucumber slices, tomato wedges, lettuce, fresh sprigs coriander and bowls of steamed rice.

Serves 4

WHOLE ROAST CHICKEN IN PEANUT COCONUT SAUCE
(GAI OB NAM KATI)

1.5 kg roasting chicken
SAUCE
1 onion, roughly chopped
2 cloves garlic, roughly chopped
1 tablespoon chopped lemon grass
4 red chillies, fresh or dried
6 tablespoons roasted peanuts or peanut paste
1 teaspoon pepper
1 tablespoon sugar
2 tablespoons fish sauce
1 teaspoon shrimp paste
1 tablespoon vegetable oil
1 cup (250 mL) coconut milk
GARNISH
fresh red chillies, finely sliced into rings and coriander sprigs

Place chicken on a rack in a baking dish and roast at 180°C (350°F) until tender (1½–2 hours). Prepare sauce ingredients during last 15 minutes of cooking.

In a food processor or a mortar, make a paste from onion, garlic, lemon grass, chillies, peanuts, pepper, sugar, fish sauce and shrimp paste. Fry paste in vegetable oil, in a large heavy-based saucepan, then add coconut milk. Stir well and simmer for 5 minutes or so until sauce is thick enough to coat chicken.

Place roasted chicken into the saucepan and carefully coat with sauce. Simmer a few minutes more but be careful not to break up the chicken. Remove to a serving plate and spoon over remaining sauce. Cover with chilli rings and coriander sprigs.

Serves 4

Duck Casserole served whole with eggs, carrots and mushrooms. The eggs can be halved or served whole.

1. Stir-fry curry paste, chilli and lime leaves.

2. Add chicken and simmer to reduce sauce.

3. Add vegetables when chicken is cooked and sauce is the desired consistency.

GREEN SWEET CHICKEN CURRY
(GAENG KEOW WAN GAI)

If you want to prepare this spicy sweet curry in advance, add the vegetables just before serving. This recipe is quick because it uses small, bite-sized pieces of chicken meat, however, you can use a whole chicken or chicken pieces with bones. Simply simmer the chicken in coconut milk with a little water, then proceed with the recipe, adding the pre-cooked and drained chicken pieces instead of raw chicken. Liquid can be added if you prefer a thinner sauce. This recipe can also be made with beef, pork or fish, but is particularly nice with poultry.

2 tablespoons vegetable oil
1½ tablespoons green curry paste, bought or homemade (see recipe)
1 fresh green chilli, finely sliced
4 dried Kaffir lime leaves, pre-soaked for ten minutes, then sliced
3 cups (750 mL) coconut milk
1 tablespoon fish sauce
2 teaspoons sugar
500 g raw chicken meat, cut into bite-sized pieces
30 g drained canned bamboo shoots, sliced zucchini or eggplant
30 g fresh or frozen peas or pea aubergines (see Ingredients)
1 tablespoon fresh basil leaves, mint or young citrus leaves

In a large saucepan, briefly stir-fry curry paste, chilli and lime leaves in oil over a medium heat, then add coconut milk, fish sauce and sugar. When coconut milk begins to bubble, add chicken and, if using, bamboo shoots, turn down heat and simmer to reduce sauce. If it becomes too thick, add a little water or more coconut milk.

When chicken is cooked and sauce is desired consistency, add peas and optional zucchini or eggplant, cooking briefly to retain their firmness. Remove from heat and stir in basil leaves, leaving a few for garnishing. Serve with rice.

Serves 4

SLICED CHICKEN WITH CHILLIES AND CASHEWS
(GAI PAD MET MAMUANG)

4 tablespoons vegetable oil
6 whole small dried red chillies
1 clove garlic, chopped
300 g lean chicken, sliced
1 tablespoon oyster sauce
1 tablespoon fish sauce
½ teaspoon sugar
1 teaspoon roasted chilli paste, bought or homemade (see recipe)
3 tablespoons Thai Soup Stock (see recipe) or water
50 g roasted, unsalted cashew nuts
2 shallots, cut in 2.5 cm pieces

Using 1 tablespoon vegetable oil in a wok, stir-fry whole chillies until cooked evenly but not burnt. Remove and put aside.

Stir-fry garlic in the remaining vegetable oil, until golden. Add chicken slices, oyster and fish sauces, sugar and roasted chilli paste and stir-fry until chicken is golden. Lower heat, add stock and cook another few minutes, stirring occasionally. When chicken is thoroughly cooked, add cashew nuts, shallots and whole chillies, and stir several times. Remove from heat and serve. You can feature whole chillies by arranging them on top of the dish.

Serves 4

CRISP FRIED SALTY CHICKEN
(GAI KEM)

1.5 kg roasting chicken
1.25 litres water
3 tablespoons coarse or cooking salt
½ cup (125 mL) vegetable oil for shallow-frying
fresh coriander sprigs, to garnish

Place chicken in large saucepan with water and bring to the boil. Simmer, loosely covered, for about 15 minutes until almost tender. Drain, reserving stock for later use, and cool. Cut chicken into four pieces, then rub well with salt. Refrigerate overnight in a covered bowl.

Pat dry then fry each side in hot oil until golden, turning when necessary. Chop into smaller pieces, if desired, and serve with hot spicy dishes like curries, to counter the chilli. Garnish with coriander sprigs.

Serves 4

STIR-FRIED GINGER CHICKEN
(PAD KING GAI)

2 tablespoons vegetable oil
1 clove garlic, finely chopped
2 tablespoons sliced ginger root, cut into fine matchsticks
200 g lean chicken, sliced into strips
1 tablespoon oyster sauce
1 tablespoon fish sauce
½ teaspoon sugar
pinch white pepper
2 shallots, cut in 2.5 cm pieces
1 onion, sliced
½ red capsicum, cut in strips
4 tablespoons dried wood fungus or mushrooms (see Note)
2 teaspoons finely chopped fresh coriander leaves, to garnish

Heat oil in wok or frypan and fry garlic and ginger until golden. Add chicken and stir-fry until golden. You may have to wait for moisture in chicken to evaporate, then it will lightly brown. Add oyster and fish sauces, sugar and pepper, and extra fish sauce or sugar if needed. Stir in shallots, onions, capsicum and wood fungus, stir-fry for several minutes, then remove from heat. Serve sprinkled with chopped coriander leaves.

Serves 4

Note: Presoak mushrooms for 1 hour, remove and discard stems. Alternatively, use dried Chinese or fresh mushrooms. The dried ones should be soaked for 20 minutes in warm water and the stems discarded.

TEST FOR TASTE
Thai cooks are flexible and creative — they adjust quantities of ingredients to suit their personal preference.

Always taste as you cook, to achieve a balance of sweet, hot and salty flavours that suits you.

If you want to add a little extra of some favourite ingredient such as coconut milk or coriander, go ahead and experiment. But be very wary of adding extra chillies.

Green Sweet Chicken Curry — Thais often serve their curries with a little less meat and vegetables and more liquid to flavour their rice.

DUCK STEAMED WITH CHINESE MELON AND PICKLED LIMES
(PED THOON MANAO DONG)

This dish falls somewhere between a soup and a casserole. You can serve it in place of a soup at dinner, or it can be a meal in itself. The Thais believe it has excellent medicinal qualities.

If you can't find Chinese green melon (Fak-keow) at your local Chinatown, substitute chokos, or any similar bitter green vegetable. You can buy Thai pickled limes, sometimes called pickled lemons, in jars at Asian stores. Don't throw out the liquid and try not to break the skin of the fruit in the casserole/soup when serving, but warn your guests they're an acquired taste.

1.5 kg young duck
1 large Chinese melon, gourd or 3 chokos
30 g Chinese dried mushrooms, soaked in water 30 minutes, stems discarded
2 tablespoons vegetable oil
3 pickled limes and ½ cup (125 mL) pickled lime liquid
1 small onion, halved
1 teaspoon white pepper
½ cup (125 mL) fish sauce

Cut duck into 5 cm pieces with cleaver and put aside. Peel melon and cut in half lengthways, then cut into 5 cm pieces and set aside. If mushrooms are uniformly large leave them, but if they come in a variety of sizes, cut the larger ones in half.

In a large heavy-based saucepan that has a lid, heat oil and add duck. Brown duck and discard excess fat and oil. Add about 2.5 litres water, the pickled limes and liquid and bring to the boil. Add extra water to ensure duck is covered by at least 3 cm liquid. Cover, allowing a small amount of steam to escape, and simmer gently for about 30 minutes, adding more water if necessary to keep duck covered. Skim surface to keep broth clear.

When duck is tender, add onion, mushrooms, melon pieces, pepper and fish sauce. Cook for another 5 minutes, check taste to see if extra pickled lime liquid, fish sauce or water is needed. Serve in a large casserole dish or tureen.

Serves 4

Chicken Salad with Mint, Onion and Lemon Grass, and Spicy Chicken Livers.

CHICKEN AND PEANUT CURRY
(GAENG PANANG GAI)

3 tablespoons vegetable oil
3 tablespoons Panang or red curry paste (Panang Curry Paste can be bought in cans or jars in Asian stores)
2 cups (500 mL) coconut milk
500 g chicken fillets, cut into bite-sized pieces
2 tablespoons sugar
2 tablespoons fish sauce
1 tablespoon dried Kaffir lime leaves, soaked for 10 minutes and cut into strips
100 g roasted peanuts, blended to a paste with 3 tablespoons coconut milk
pinch cumin, coriander or salt
2 tablespoons whole basil leaves

In a wok or frypan over a medium heat, stir-fry curry paste in oil, then add ½ cup (125 mL) coconut milk. Turn heat to low, add chicken and stir slowly until curry paste is blended well and flavours combine.

Add another cup (250 mL) coconut milk, then sugar, fish sauce, lime leaves and bring sauce to the boil. Simmer for a few minutes, add peanut and coconut milk paste, stir, and pour in remaining coconut milk.

Simmer for another 10 minutes then taste. The curry should be sweet, spicy and a little salty. If necessary add a little more sugar, cumin, coriander or salt. Gaeng Panang curries should be a golden red colour with oily patterns on the surface. The sauce should be about half as thick as satay sauce, which is why the dish is often called 'dry' chicken curry. Garnish with basil leaves and serve with rice.

Serves 4

SPICY CHICKEN LIVERS
(THAB GAI PAD PRIKON)

300 g chicken livers
6 dried Chinese mushrooms, soaked for 20 minutes in hot water
2 tablespoons vegetable oil
1 clove garlic, finely chopped
2 medium-sized onions, sliced
2 fresh red chillies, finely sliced
2 tablespoons fish sauce
1 teaspoon sugar
2 tablespoons lemon juice
½ green capsicum, sliced
3 shallots, cut in 3 cm pieces

Wash and dry chicken livers, and cut into bite-sized pieces. Finely slice mushrooms, removing stems. Set aside.

Heat oil in wok or frypan and stir-fry garlic until golden, then add onions and chillies and stir-fry for 1 minute. Add chicken livers, stir-fry until just pink, then add fish sauce, sugar, lemon juice and mushrooms. Stir-fry for another minute and check taste to see if more fish sauce, sugar or lemon juice is needed. Stir in capsicum and shallots, stir-fry another minute and serve with rice.

Serves 4

CHICKEN SALAD WITH MINT, ONION AND LEMON GRASS
(LAAB GAI)

200 g lean chicken meat, minced
1 tablespoon fish sauce
1 tablespoon finely chopped lemon grass
3 tablespoons water or chicken Thai Soup Stock (see recipe)
1½ tablespoons lemon juice
1 onion, finely sliced
1 tablespoon chopped shallots
1 tablespoon finely chopped coriander
4 tablespoons fresh mint leaves
2 tablespoons rice, dry-fried to golden, then ground
1 teaspoon chilli powder (optional)
GARNISH
lettuce leaves, fresh mint and coriander leaves, chilli flowers and shallot curls (see recipes)

In a saucepan over medium heat, gently cook minced chicken, fish sauce and lemon grass with the water, stirring to separate the chicken mince to an even texture. If necessary, add a little more water to keep about 3 tablespoons of liquid in the pan. Remove from heat after 5 minutes or so, when chicken is cooked through but still moist.

Add lemon juice, onion, shallots, coriander and mint leaves and toss gently. Taste to see if extra fish sauce or lemon juice is needed. Sprinkle in golden ground rice and toss again gently. If you want the dish to be spicy, add chilli powder or, alternatively, serve some in a side bowl.

Serve on a bed of lettuce leaves and garnish. Serve at room temperature or slightly chilled.

Serves 4

1. *Prepare quail by washing, cleaning and patting dry.*

2. *Remove internal bone and cut in half lengthways.*

3. *Cut each half into 3 pieces.*

QUAIL WITH CHILLI AND BASIL
(NOK PAD PRIK)

4 average-sized quail
1 cup (250 mL) vegetable oil
2 cloves garlic, chopped
4 fresh chillies (moderately hot), sliced
1 tablespoon oyster sauce
2 tablespoons fish sauce
1 tablespoon roasted chilli paste, bought or homemade (see recipe)
2 tablespoons fresh whole basil leaves

Wash and clean quail, pat dry, then with a smooth-faced mallet, gently soften and flatten them. Remove internal bone and cut quail in half lengthways, then cut each half into three pieces. In a wok, fry quail pieces in hot oil until cooked, about 5 minutes. Remove and put aside.

Leave 3 tablespoons oil in the wok, and reserve the remainder for later use (for another dish). Stir-fry garlic until golden, add chillies, quail, oyster and fish sauces and roasted chilli paste. If necessary, add a little water or stock to moisten. Stir-fry for a few minutes, then taste and add more chilli or fish sauce, if desired. Stir basil leaves through mixture, then remove from heat. Serve with rice.

Serves 4

THAI BARBECUED CHICKEN
(GAI YAHNG)

1 kg chicken pieces, slightly larger than bite-sized (see *Note*)
MARINADE
1 tablespoon chopped coriander root and stem
1 tablespoon chopped garlic
1 teaspoon pepper
1 teaspoon sugar
1 teaspoon salt
2 teaspoons ground turmeric
3 tablespoons vegetable oil

Combine all marinade ingredients in a food processor or crush with a mortar and pestle. Rub chicken pieces with marinade, and leave covered for at least 10 minutes, or preferably overnight, in the refrigerator.

Barbecue over hot coals or grill slowly until thoroughly cooked and slightly charred. Serve with a spicy Thai sauce and rice.

Note: You can barbecue large chicken pieces and chop into smaller pieces with a mallet before serving, or split the larger limbs and slightly flatten them, so they cook easily.

Serves 4

CHICKEN AND COCONUT MILK CASSEROLE
(GAENG TOM KAH GAI)

3 cups (750 mL) coconut milk
1 cup (250 mL) water or chicken stock
2 tablespoons fish sauce
2 tablespoons chopped coriander roots
8 pieces dried galangal
1 teaspoon finely sliced lemon grass bulb
1 tablespoon sliced lemon grass stalk, cut in 2.5 cm pieces
8 dried Kaffir lime leaves
½ teaspoon white pepper
1.5 kg chicken pieces, chopped into 5 cm pieces with bones
3 teaspoons roasted chilli paste or 1 teaspoon fresh chopped or dried chilli
2 teaspoons sugar
2 tablespoons lemon juice
100g whole button mushrooms, fresh or canned (see *Note*)
chopped fresh coriander, to garnish

Credit: Dansab; Lifestyle Imports

Put coconut milk, water, fish sauce, coriander root, galangal, lemon grass, lime leaves and pepper in a large saucepan and bring to the boil. Reduce heat, add chicken and simmer for about 20 minutes, adding more water if necessary.

Add roasted chilli paste, sugar and lemon juice, simmer for another minute and taste to see if extra fish sauce, sugar, lemon juice or chilli paste is needed. When chicken is tender, add mushrooms and cook for 3 minutes. Garnish with chopped coriander leaves and serve with steamed rice.

Serves 4

Note: You can also add zucchini, eggplant, bamboo shoots or green peas if you like, at the same time as the mushrooms.

STEAMED SPICY CHICKEN (HAW MOK GAI)

300 g lean chicken, minced or finely chopped
2 tablespoons green curry paste, bought or homemade (see recipe)
2 tablespoons fish sauce
1 cup (250 mL) coconut milk
4 tablespoons shredded coconut
2 dried Kaffir lime leaves, soaked for 10 minutes and shredded
1 teaspoon pepper
1 egg, beaten
200–300 g sliced Chinese cabbage, spinach or leeks (any combination)
½ cup (125 mL) thick coconut cream, skimmed from top of canned coconut milk before it's shaken
fresh coriander sprigs, to garnish

Combine minced chicken with curry paste, fish sauce, coconut milk, shredded coconut, lime leaves, pepper and beaten egg. Taste to see if extra seasoning is required as you can't stir in more flavours once steaming has begun.

Line a baking dish that will fit inside a steamer with banana leaves or aluminium foil. Place a layer of green vegetables over the bottom and cover with the chicken mixture. Top with thick coconut cream, garnish with coriander sprigs and steam for 20–30 minutes.

Serves 4

Quail with Chilli and Basil and Thai Barbecued Chicken. Serve the chicken with any of the spicy hot Thai sauces.

SALADS

A Thai meal will invariably include at least one salad. Often Thai salads have small quantities of meat and fish to flavour or contrast with the vegetables — flaked fish, ground dried shrimp or minced pork. So these recipes can be thought of as side dishes and accompaniments to a main meal, or as a perfect light lunch or supper.

Don't toss all your ingredients together. Arrange them neatly on a platter with an eye to their colours and shapes. Don't crowd too many ingredients into one salad and, if you can, decorate your creations with a chilli flower or a tomato basket or two for special dinners (see recipes), and do mention to dinner guests not to eat the chilli flower!

GREEN MANGO SALAD
(YAM MAMUANG)

Green mangoes aren't always available, so this salad can be made with tart green apples instead. The fruit makes a surprising contrast with the rich pork and peanut sauce.

4 large green mangoes or cooking
  apples, peeled, cored and sliced
4 tablespoons lemon juice
1 tablespoon vegetable oil
3 cloves garlic, finely chopped
2 onions, finely sliced
200 g minced pork
3 tablespoons fish sauce
1 tablespoon sugar
½ teaspoon white pepper
1 tablespoon ground dried shrimp
4 tablespoons ground peanuts or
  crunchy peanut butter
1 teaspoon finely sliced fresh chilli
  (optional)
1 teaspoon dried chilli flakes, optional
  (see recipe)
6 lettuce leaves, to serve

Sprinkle mango with lemon juice and marinate for 5 minutes. In a wok or frypan, fry garlic in oil until golden, then add onions and fry until clear. Remove with a slotted spoon and set aside on absorbent kitchen paper. Add minced pork to wok and stir-fry until almost cooked. Stir in fish sauce, sugar, pepper, ground dried shrimps, peanuts and chilli, if using. Cook for another few minutes then remove from heat.

Combine mango slices with onion and garlic, and then the peanut-pork mixture, adding dried chilli flakes if desired. Toss gently, then chill. Serve on a bed of lettuce leaves, with garnishes of your choice.

Serves 4

PRAWN SALAD WITH LEMON GRASS AND MINT
(YAM PLA GOONG)

400 g green (uncooked) prawns,
  shelled, deveined, tails intact (see
  Note)
2 tablespoons lemon juice
1½ tablespoons fish sauce
1 tablespoon roasted chilli paste,
  bought or homemade (see recipe),
  optional
3 tablespoons water
2 onions, finely sliced or in rings
2 tablespoons chopped shallots
2 tablespoons thinly sliced lemon
  grass
3 tablespoons chopped fresh mint
  leaves
2 tablespoons chopped fresh coriander
1 teaspoon finely chopped fresh chilli
  (optional)
4 lettuce leaves, to serve

Place prawns, lemon juice, fish sauce, roasted chilli paste and water in a saucepan, stir, and heat slowly until prawns turn pink. Taste to see if extra lemon juice or fish sauce is needed. Remove from heat and add onions, shallots, lemon grass, mint, coriander and fresh chilli, if using. Toss gently and serve on a bed of lettuce leaves. Garnish as you wish.

Serves 4

Note: This salad is equally, if not more, delicious made with lobster tails, tails of Balmain bugs, butterfly lobsters, Moreton Bay bugs, crayfish or any other favourite seafood.

Green Mango Salad, and Prawn Salad with Lemon Grass and Mint. If you prefer you can achieve a moist and milder prawn salad by only slightly braising the prawns until they just turn pink, and adding only a hint of chilli.

Credit: Made Where

CARROT AND GREEN BEAN SALAD WITH PAWPAW
(SOM TAM)

Som Tam literally means 'sour and pounded', and that's what is so unusual about this dish. The salad has a slight tartness from the lemon juice and it's bruised or lightly pounded to a soft, but never mushy, consistency. Serve Som Tam on a bed of lettuce leaves and with a plate of Spicy Minced Beef or Chicken Salad with Mint, Onion and Lemon Grass (see recipes).

3 cloves garlic, peeled
1 teaspoon sliced fresh or dried chilli (optional)
100 g stringless green beans, cut into 2.5 cm pieces
2 medium-sized carrots, shredded
2 medium-sized red tomatoes, diced
1 small green pawpaw, peeled, seeded and diced in 2 cm cubes (optional)
½ cup (125 mL) lemon juice
3 tablespoons fish sauce
1 tablespoon sugar
5 tablespoons dried shrimp, washed, then ground
2 tablespoons crushed roasted peanuts
4 lettuce leaves, to serve

Using a mortar and pestle, pound garlic and chilli until well pulverised. Remove and place in a large plastic mixing bowl, with beans. Slightly bruise them with a pestle, add carrot and tomato, bruise them, then add green pawpaw and again, lightly bruise.

Add about 4 tablespoons of the lemon juice, add the fish sauce and sugar and toss with a large spoon. Taste and if necessary add more chilli, sugar, lemon juice or fish sauce.

When satisfied with the flavour and consistency, sprinkle with ground shrimp and toss again. Serve sprinkled with ground peanuts, on a bed of lettuce leaves, with garnishes of your choice.

Serves 4

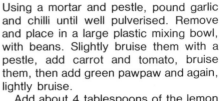

Credit: Dansab

SPICY MINCED BEEF
(LAAB NUA)

Laab nua, sometimes called laab issan, is a Thai version of steak tartare and is thought to have come from the Mongols, or Tartars as they were sometimes called, when the T'ai lived in the Yunnan Valley region more than 1000 years ago.

200 g lean beef, minced or finely chopped
3 tablespoons water
1 tablespoon lemon juice
1 tablespoon fish sauce
1 large onion, finely sliced
1 tablespoon finely chopped shallots
2 tablespoons rice, dry-fried and ground
4 tablespoons fresh mint leaves
1 tablespoon finely chopped fresh coriander stem and leaves
1 tablespoon finely sliced lemon grass
½ teaspoon chilli powder or finely chopped fresh chilli

GARNISH
fresh basil leaves, coriander leaves, mint leaves, shallot curls and chilli flowers (see recipes), lettuce leaves, snake beans or sliced cucumber (any combination)

In a saucepan, braise beef in water using a wooden spoon to separate, until beef is medium-rare and still quite pink. Remove from heat and combine with lemon juice, fish sauce, onion, shallots, ground rice, mint leaves, coriander, lemon grass and chilli powder. Place in a mound on a bed of lettuce leaves and decorate with garnishes of your choice.

Serves 4

Carrot and Green Bean Salad with Pawpaw. If using dried shrimp whole, soak them in warm water for 20 minutes then pound them; but they're best ground.

PRAWN AND ORANGE SALAD
(GOONG SOD GUP SOM KEOW WAN)

300 g green (uncooked) prawns,
  peeled, deveined, with tails intact (if
  large)
1 tablespoon roasted chilli paste,
  bought or homemade (see recipe),
  optional
2 tablespoons lemon juice
1½ tablespoons fish sauce
3 tablespoons water
1 onion, sliced into fine rings
1 teaspoon finely sliced fresh chilli
  (optional)
4 oranges, peeled, seeded and sliced
1 bunch fresh mint leaves
6 lettuce leaves, to serve

Place prawns, roasted chilli paste, lemon
juice, fish sauce and water in a saucepan, stir and heat slowly until prawns turn
pink. Remove from heat and cool.

To prawn mixture, add onion rings,
fresh chilli, if using, orange slices and
mint leaves and mix thoroughly. Serve on
a bed of lettuce leaves either chilled or at
room temperature, with garnishes of your
choice.

Serves 4

GLASS NOODLE SALAD
(YAM WOON SEN)

200 g lean chicken or pork, minced, or
  200 g whole green (uncooked)
  prawns, peeled
3 tablespoons or more chicken Thai
  Soup Stock (see recipe)
1½ tablespoons lemon juice
1 tablespoon fish sauce
1 tablespoon roasted chilli paste,
  bought or homemade (see recipe)
100 g cellophane noodles, soaked in
  warm water for 10 minutes and
  drained
1 large onion, sliced
2 tablespoons chopped shallots
2 tablespoons chopped fresh coriander
2 tablespoons fresh mint leaves
6 lettuce leaves or Chinese cabbage
  leaves, to serve

In a saucepan over medium heat, braise
meat in stock for several minutes, then
add lemon juice, fish sauce and roasted
chilli paste. Cook another few minutes.

Add half the drained noodles and toss
gently, making sure mixture remains
moist. Add remaining noodles and a little
more stock if necessary. Taste to see if
extra seasoning is required; if you want it
more spicy, add a little more roasted chilli
paste or some dried or fresh chilli.

When satisfied with the flavour and
consistency, add onion, shallots, coriander and mint, and toss gently. Serve on
a bed of lettuce.

Serves 4

Credit: Dansab; Made in Japan Imports

*Glass Noodle Salad can be made with
prawns, chicken or pork or all three. Toss
gently so the noodles don't become
soggy.*

GREAT SALAD
(YAM YAI)

6 lettuce leaves (Chinese preferably)
100 g any cooked meat, seafood slices
   or beancurd cubes (optional)
3 large tomatoes, cut into wedges
1 large cucumber, peeled and sliced
   (with some skin for colour)
100 g blanched broccoli florets
½ red capsicum, cut in strips
2 medium-sized onions, finely sliced
   into rings
6 shallot curls (see recipe)
3 hard-boiled eggs, peeled and halved

GARNISH
1 sliced hard-boiled egg, fresh
   coriander leaves and chilli flowers
   (see recipe)

DRESSING
80 g unsalted roasted peanuts
½ cup (125 mL) lemon juice
3 tablespoons vinegar
4 cloves garlic
3 tablespoons chopped coriander
   plant, including root
3 tablespoons sugar
1 tablespoon salt
1 tablespoon fish sauce
1 whole fresh chilli (optional)
3 tablespoons water or more

Blend all dressing ingredients in a food processor or blender, using water to achieve the consistency you prefer. Add even more water if you like a thinner dressing. Taste to see if you need extra vinegar, sugar or fish sauce.

On a large platter, carefully arrange salad ingredients on a bed of lettuce leaves with an eye for colour contrast. Pour dressing over salad (as much as you like, reserving some for future use if you want to), then garnish with sliced egg, coriander leaves and chilli flowers. Serve slightly chilled or at room temperature.

Serves 4

1. Prepare all ingredients first — peeling, chopping and slicing as required.

2. Make dressing

3. Carefully arrange ingredients on bed of lettuce.

4. Garnish to serve with sliced eggs, coriander leaves and chilli flowers.

SPICY FISH SALAD
(MIANG PLA)

1½ cups (375 mL) water
3 tablespoons coarse salt
500 g whole snapper, tailor, kingfish or mackerel
2 tablespoons sliced fresh ginger root
3 cloves garlic, finely sliced
2 tablespoons chopped shallots
3 medium-sized onions, finely sliced
2 tablespoons chopped coriander leaves
1 tablespoon dried chillies, fried in oil and drained
1 teaspoon finely sliced fresh chilli
1 tablespoon fresh mint leaves
1 tablespoon finely chopped lemon grass
2 tablespoons roasted peanuts
2 tablespoons lemon juice
1½ tablespoons fish sauce
4 large lettuce leaves, to serve

GARNISH
2 tablespoons roasted peanuts, 1 tablespoon finely sliced ginger root, dried and fresh chilli, lemon wedges, coriander leaves, chilli flowers and shallot curls (see recipes)

Mix water and coarse salt, pour over fish and soak overnight in a dish in the refrigerator. Remove and drain fish, then steam or grill it. Cool and carefully flake with a fork.

Place flaked fish in a large mixing bowl with ginger, garlic, shallots, onions, coriander leaves, chillies, mint leaves, lemon grass and roasted peanuts. Add the lemon juice and fish sauce and lightly toss.

Serve on a bed of lettuce leaves, garnished with mounds of peanuts, ginger, and dried and fresh chilli, around the rim of the plate. Decorate with remaining garnish ingredients.

Serves 4

BEEF SALAD WITH CHILLI, ONION AND CUCUMBER
(YAM NUA)

200 g lean beef, 3 cm thick steaks of fillet or rump
2 tablespoons water
1 tablespoon lemon juice
1 tablespoon fish sauce
1 medium-sized cucumber, sliced
1 large onion, sliced
1 tablespoon chopped shallots
½ teaspoon fresh or dried chilli (optional)
1 tablespoon chopped fresh coriander leaves
2 tablespoons fresh mint leaves
6 lettuce leaves, to serve
garnishes of your choice

Tenderise beef with a mallet if necessary, then barbecue or grill to medium-rare. Cut into fine thin slices about 5 cm × 1 cm. Place beef in a saucepan or wok over medium heat and braise briefly in 2 tablespoons water, so water absorbs meat flavour. Don't overcook meat.

Remove from heat and add lemon juice, fish sauce, cucumber, onion, shallots, chilli, coriander and mint. Stir, then place on a bed of lettuce leaves and surround the beef salad with an interesting assortment of colourful garnishes of your choice.

Serves 4

CALAMARI SALAD WITH MINT, ONION AND LEMON GRASS
(YAM PLA MEUK)

200 g calamari tubes
3 tablespoons water
1½ tablespoons fish sauce
1½ tablespoons lemon juice
1 tablespoon roasted chilli paste or 1 teaspoon fresh chopped chilli (optional)
1 meduim-sized onion, sliced or in fine rings
1 tablespoon chopped shallots
1 tablespoon finely chopped lemon grass
1 tablespoon chopped fresh coriander leaves
1 tablespoon fresh mint leaves
1 tablespoon ground rice, dry-fried until golden
6 lettuce leaves, to serve
5 sprigs fresh coriander

Wash and drain calamari tubes. Score in a crosshatch pattern and cut into 4 cm square pieces. Calamari pieces are usually much more tender than ready-cut rings.

In a saucepan over medium heat, bring the water to the boil. Add calamari pieces, fish sauce, lemon juice and roasted chilli paste and stir until cooked and tender. Depending on how young the calamari are, it will take 5–20 minutes. Check constantly after several minutes, as calamari can cook quickly and becomes tough when overcooked.

Taste to see if extra fish sauce, lemon juice or chilli paste is needed to balance flavours, then remove from heat. Stir in onion, shallots, lemon grass, coriander, mint leaves and ground rice. Toss gently and serve, either warm or cooled, on a bed of lettuce leaves garnished with coriander sprigs.

Serves 4

Cucumbers are a vital ingredient in Thai cuisine.

CUCUMBER SALAD
(YAM THANG KWA)

2 medium-sized cucumbers, peeled, seeded and diced
2 tablespoons finely chopped onion
2 tablespoons sliced shallots, cut into 2 cm pieces
2 tablespoons dried shrimp, washed and ground
2 tablespoons finely chopped fresh coriander stems and leaves
4 tablespoons fresh mint leaves
2 tablespoons fish sauce
4 tablespoons lemon juice
1 teaspoon sugar
6 large lettuce leaves

GARNISH
3 tablespoons crushed roasted unsalted peanuts, ½ teaspoon dried chilli flakes, mint and coriander sprigs

Drain diced cucumber on absorbent kitchen paper for a few minutes then place in a bowl and combine with onion, shallots, dried shrimp, chopped coriander and mint leaves. Sprinkle with fish sauce, lemon juice and sugar, and toss gently.

Place lettuce leaves on a platter and arrange cucumber salad in a mound on top. Sprinkle with ground peanuts and dried chilli flakes; garnish with mint and coriander sprigs.

Serves 4

CUCUMBERS
Thai cooking uses lots of cucumber — in soups and salads, and as a garnish. Use any long, green, smooth-skinned cucumber available. They go under a variety of names, depending on what part of the world you live in: English, Lebanese, Cypress or telegraph cucumbers. In most recipes, small round cucumbers, known as apple cucumbers, make an acceptable substitute, but they are not appropriate for stuffing.

Credit: Appley Hoare Antiques

ROSE PETAL AND WATERCRESS SALAD
(YAM DOK GULAB)

4 tablespoons fish sauce
4 tablespoons lemon juice
2 teaspoons sugar
100 g cooked chicken, finely sliced
100 g cooked pork, finely chopped
100 g cooked prawns, chopped
  (optional)
2 tablespoons ground roasted unsalted
  peanuts
3 cloves garlic, finely chopped, fried
  golden and drained
2 medium-sized onions, finely sliced,
  fried golden and drained
1 bunch watercress, chopped
20–30 rose petals, rinsed and drained
6 large lettuce leaves, to serve

GARNISH
**fresh mint and coriander leaves, sliced
chilli strips, chilli flowers and shallot
curls (see recipes)**

In a bowl combine fish sauce, lemon juice
and sugar. Stir until sugar dissolves. Add
chicken, pork, prawns and ground peanuts and mix well. Then add fried garlic
and onions and toss lightly. Carefully
combine with chopped watercress and
most of the rose petals, avoiding bruising
the petals.

Place in a mound on the lettuce leaves
and garnish with remaining rose petals
and other garnish ingredients attractively
arranged.

Serves 4

*Rose Petal and Watercress Salad.
Choose any colour of rose petals and if
you like the taste and colour of
watercress, add lots more. Choose rose
petals from your own garden so that you
know they haven't been sprayed.*

Vegetables and Other Side Dishes

An abundance of vegetables, raw or slightly cooked, makes Thai cuisine very nutritious. Vegetables also play an important role in balancing flavours *in a meal and providing relief for the mouth after the searing chilli dishes and spicy curries.*

CRISP DEEP-FRIED VEGETABLES
(PAK TOD)

A side dish of crisp fried vegetables coated in a feather-light batter.

variety of fresh vegetables cut in uniform sizes e.g. broccoli, cauliflower, champignons, carrot, zucchini, celery, capsicum, green beans
2 cups (500 mL) vegetable oil, for deep-frying
BATTER (see *Note*)
1 cup (125 g) cornflour
½ teaspoon salt
1 teaspoon sugar
1 teaspoon baking soda
½ cup (125 mL) vegetable oil
½ cup (125 mL) tepid water

To make batter, place cornflour, salt, sugar, baking soda, oil and some of the water in a bowl and beat lightly with a fork. Add more water if necessary to achieve a thin batter. Wait for bubbles to appear on the surface, then chill for 30 minutes.

Lightly coat vegetable pieces with the batter. Deep-fry in very hot oil until just golden. Remove and drain on absorbent kitchen paper. Skim any burnt pieces of batter from the surface of oil and take care the oil doesn't get too hot and smoke or burn. Serve with a bowl of Sweet Chilli Dipping Sauce (see recipe).

Serves 4

Note: This homemade batter may be replaced with commercial tempura mix, available at supermarkets and delicatessens.

Crisp Deep-fried Vegetables and Sweet Chilli Dipping Sauce, Stir-fried Mixed Vegetables, and Fresh Whole Coriander with Spicy Tamarind Dip.

STIR-FRIED MIXED VEGETABLES
(PAD PAK RUAM)

3 tablespoons vegetable oil
2 cloves garlic, finely chopped
400–500 g mixed vegetables e.g. Chinese cabbage, broccoli, green beans, brussels sprouts, cucumber, carrots, lettuce, cabbage, Chinese broccoli, bok choy, bean sprouts or spinach (any combination)
3 tablespoons water
1 tablespoon fish sauce
1 tablespoon oyster sauce
½ teaspoon sugar
½ teaspoon white pepper

In a wok over high heat, stir-fry garlic in oil for a few seconds, then add vegetables (except bean sprouts, if using).

Stir-fry quickly for about 1 minute while vegetables splutter noisily because of their high water content. Add water, fish and oyster sauces, sugar and pepper.

Stir quickly and cook for another 1–2 minutes, until vegetables are lightly cooked but crisp. If using bean sprouts, stir in just before you finish cooking. Remove from heat and serve.

Serves 4

FRESH WHOLE CORIANDER WITH SPICY TAMARIND DIP
(NAM PLA WAN PAK CHEE)

This is a dish for lovers of that taste so synonymous with Thai cuisine — fresh coriander. In Thailand it's not unusual to find whole coriander plants served as a side dish to a meal. Here's a recipe for a traditional sauce that has been popular for generations, one that especially complements fresh coriander, and is served at a meal with barbecued fish or prawns. The sauce should be eaten freshly made.

6 whole fresh coriander plants, roots included
3 tablespoons dried shrimp, soaked for 5 minutes and drained
2 large dried chillies, soaked 10 minutes and drained
½ cup (125 mL) tamarind juice
1 tablespoon fish sauce
2 tablespoons palm or brown sugar
1 medium-sized Spanish or brown onion, neatly sliced
2 cloves garlic, finely sliced
1 teaspoon chopped fresh coriander leaves

Prepare coriander plants by cleaning thoroughly and removing any broken or yellowing leaves (do not remove roots). Arrange on a serving plate and put aside.

Dry-fry dried shrimp in a heavy-based frypan for several minutes, then grind or pound finely. Slice chillies finely and dry-fry, seeds included. Mix in a small bowl with tamarind juice, fish sauce and sugar and stir. Taste to see if extra tamarind juice, fish sauce or sugar is needed to balance the flavours of hot, sweet, sour and salty.

Add ground shrimp, onion, garlic and coriander leaves, and stir. If necessary add a little boiled water to thin the sauce. Place in a bowl accompanied by the plate of whole coriander plants. Serve as a green salad side dish. To eat, simply break off a piece of stem or root, and dip in the sauce.

Serves 4

1. Clean coriander plants thoroughly.

2. Prepare sauce then place in a bowl and serve with whole coriander plants.

PICKLED VEGETABLES
(PAK DONG)

3 cups (750 mL) white vinegar
1½ tablespoons sugar
2 teaspoons salt
250 g cauliflower pieces
250 g cucumber, peeled, seeded and
　diced
250 g baby corn
100 g carrots, sliced
100 g broccoli, bok choy or Chinese
　broccoli pieces
200 g cabbage, cut into pieces
4 cloves garlic, finely chopped
1 medium-sized onion, finely chopped
6 dried red chillies, seeded and
　chopped
1 cup (250 mL) peanut oil
1 tablespoon sesame seeds, dry-fried
　to golden, and fresh coriander
　leaves, to garnish

In a large saucepan, bring vinegar, sugar and salt to the boil. Add all the vegetables (except garlic, onion and chillies) and blanch for about 1 minute, ensuring they remain crisp. The leafy vegetables will probably need less cooking time, so use your discretion. Remove from heat and put aside, leaving vegetables to stand in the vinegar syrup.

In a food processor, combine the garlic, onion and chillies and blend to a smooth paste. In a wok or large frypan, heat oil and stir-fry paste for several minutes, then add blanched vegetables and their syrup. Stir and cook for about 1 minute, combining flavours but being careful not to break up the vegetables or overcook them.

Serve warm on a dish sprinkled with roasted sesame seeds and garnished with coriander, or cool and pour into sterilised jars for later use. If covered tightly, jars can be stored for a week or two.

Serves 4

1. *In a large saucepan, bring vinegar, sugar and salt to the boil and add vegetables.*

2. Stir-fry the paste.

3. Serve warm sprinkled with sesame seeds.

4. Pour into sterilised jars. If covered tightly, Pickled Vegetables will keep for 1–2 weeks.

Stir-fried Asparagus

PICKLED GARLIC
(GRATEUM DONG)

1 cup (250 mL) white vinegar
1 litre water
3 tablespoons sugar
1 tablespoon salt
6 bulbs garlic (about 100 cloves),
   peeled unless skin is really tender
3 × 300 mL screw-top jars, cleaned
   and sterilised

In a saucepan, bring vinegar, water, sugar and salt to the boil. Reduce heat and simmer for about 5 minutes. Add garlic and boil for another minute or so, then remove from heat. Cool and pour into the sterilised jars. Keeps for months in the refrigerator, but wait at least a week before eating, for the full flavour to develop.

Makes about 3 × 300 mL jars

PICKLED LEMONS OR LIMES
(MANAO DONG)

10 small (unripe) green lemons or limes
180 g salt
750 mL–1 litre water
1 tablespoon sugar

Choose smooth-skinned lemons that are not too young and pithy. Roll each lemon on a flat surface with a plate for several minutes to soften. Then rub skin well with dampened salt to coat them and leave overnight. If it's sunny, leave them in the sun for a few hours the following day. Boil the water, salt and sugar for 5 minutes, then allow to cool. Place lemons in sterilised jars and pour salty water over them. Seal and do not use for at least 3 months. Will keep indefinitely.

Makes 2 × 300 mL jars

SALTED EGGS
(KAI KEM)

375 g salt
2–2.5 litres water
12 eggs

Bring salt and water to the boil. Remove from heat and cool until lukewarm. Place eggs carefully in a large glass or earthenware jar. Pour the brine over them until eggs are completely covered. Seal the jar and stand in a cool place for at least 1 month.

Makes 1 dozen

MIXED VEGETABLES IN COCONUT SAUCE
(PAK TOM KATI)

1 cup (250 mL) coconut milk
1 tablespoon fish sauce
2 teaspoons sugar
2 dried Kaffir lime leaves, soaked for
   5 minutes in hot water (optional)
½ teaspoon pepper
1 tablespoon sliced onion
1 fresh red chilli, finely sliced
   (optional)
100 g peas
100 g sliced green beans
30 g mushrooms, sliced
60 g eggplant, thickly sliced
100 g English spinach, chopped
100 g Chinese cabbage, shredded

In a saucepan, bring coconut milk, fish sauce, sugar, lime leaves and pepper to the boil. Reduce heat, add onion and simmer for 2 minutes. Taste to see if more sugar or fish sauce is needed. Add vegetables, the leafier ones last, and simmer until the vegetables are just cooked. Serve with rice or noodles.

Serves 4

STIR-FRIED ASPARAGUS
(PAD NAW MAI FARANG)

2 tablespoons vegetable oil
2 cloves garlic, finely chopped
400 g fresh asparagus, sliced into
   5 cm pieces
2 tablespoons oyster sauce
1 tablespoon fish sauce
1 teaspoon white pepper
1 teaspoon sugar

Heat oil in a wok or frypan, and stir-fry garlic until golden. Add asparagus and stir-fry for 1 minute. Then add oyster and fish sauces, pepper and sugar. Stir a few times, then taste. Add extra seasoning if needed. Stir-fry another 1–2 minutes then remove from heat and serve.

Serves 4

PORK STUFFED OMELETTE
(KAI YAD SAI MUU SAB)

2 tablespoons vegetable oil
1 small clove garlic, finely chopped
1 small onion, finely chopped
2 tablespoons finely chopped
    coriander root
100 g lean pork, minced
1 medium-sized tomato, chopped
60 g snow peas, green beans or
    capsicum, finely chopped
1 teaspoon sugar
1 teaspoon pepper
½ tablespoon fish sauce
4 eggs, lightly beaten with 1
    tablespoon fish sauce
chopped fresh coriander leaves, to
    garnish

In a wok or frypan, using half the oil, stir-fry garlic until golden, add onion and coriander root and stir-fry for another minute. Add minced pork and stir-fry until brown, then add tomato and green vegetables.

Cook several minutes, season with sugar, pepper and fish sauce, taste for flavour, then remove from heat.

In an omelette pan or frypan, heat remaining tablespoon of oil over medium heat and pour in egg and fish sauce mixture. When omelette begins to set, put pork and vegetable mixture in the centre and fold sides of omelette over to form a square. When omelette is golden underneath, turn it over like a pancake and brown on the other side.

Can be served as a square, or sliced into serving portions. If individual omelettes are preferred, simply cook in smaller quantities. Garnish with chopped coriander leaves.

Serves 4

Pork Stuffed Omelette

1. *Make filling in a wok then remove from heat.*

2. *Cook omelette in an omelette pan or frypan.*

3. *When omelette begins to set, add filling and fold over.*

DESSERTS AND THAI SWEETS

Credit: Made in Japan Imports

Thai cuisine is rich in sweets and desserts but they're not always served after a meal. They are often reserved for banquets, special meals and festive occasions. The usual finale to a meal in Thailand is a platter of fresh fruit (Ponlamai), artistically arranged and often skilfully carved into decorative shapes. Use your favourite fruit in season.

Many Thai sweets sold by street vendors do make wonderful desserts — the simplest of them all, sticky rice and mango, is hard to beat.

MANGOES WITH STICKY RICE
(MAMUANG KHAO NIEO)

This is one of the most famous Thai 'desserts', eaten as a snack day and night in Thailand. It's sold wrapped in a banana leaf from roadside vendors and also adorns the menus of some of the most expensive Bangkok restaurants. It's the perfect finale to a Thai feast and will have your guests begging for more.

375 g freshly made cooked sticky rice
   (see recipe)
1 cup (250 mL) thick coconut milk
4 tablespoons sugar
2 teaspoons salt
4 tablespoons coconut cream,
   skimmed from top of coconut milk
roasted seasame seeds, to garnish
6 large ripe mangoes, peeled, halved,
   stoned

Make sticky rice according to recipe; place in a bowl and set aside. In a saucepan over medium heat, bring coconut milk, sugar and salt to the boil, lower heat and simmer until milk thickens, about 4–5 minutes.

Pour mixture carefully over sticky rice, fluffing up rice with a fork and allowing coconut mixture to trickle through but not 'drown' the rice (otherwise it becomes too gluggy and you lose the lovely translucent quality of the sticky rice).

Allow rice to stand for 10 minutes, then turn out in a mound on a serving platter. Garnish with thick coconut cream sprinkled with sesame seeds.

Slice mangoes and arrange around the mound of sticky rice. Alternatively, make individual servings of sticky rice and mango slices.

Serves 4–6

MANGO ICE CREAM
(ICE CREAM MAMUANG)

4 ripe mangoes or 400–500 g canned
   sliced mango
¾ cup (180 g) sugar (½ cup (125 g) if
   using canned mango)
1 tablespoon lemon juice
1 tablespoon gelatine, dissolved in
   3 tablespoons water
1½ cups (375 mL) thickened cream,
   whipped until stiff
extra mango slices and fresh mint
   sprigs, to garnish

Peel, seed and cut mangoes. Place in a bowl and then add sugar, lemon juice and dissolved gelatine. Mix well until sugar dissolves. Fold whipped cream into mango mixture.

Spoon into a metal tray, place in the coldest part of the freezer until half frozen, then remove. Place in a food processor or chilled bowl and beat until smooth. Return to freezer tray and freeze completely. Serve with fresh sliced ripe mango, garnished with mint sprigs.

Serves 4

Mangoes with Sticky Rice garnished with thick coconut cream and roasted sesame seeds, and Mango Ice Cream garnished with a mint sprig.

THAI FRIED BANANAS
(GLUAY TOD)

4 large firm bananas, peeled
40 g butter
5 tablespoons brown sugar
4 tablespoons lemon or lime juice

Slice bananas lengthways, then cut in half to make four equal pieces. Heat butter in a wok over medium heat and fry bananas on both sides until golden.

Add sugar and stir gently until sugar dissolves and turns into a syrup. Remove from heat to a serving bowl, sprinkle with lemon juice and serve.

Serves 4

ORANGES IN ROSE OR JASMINE SYRUP
(SOM NAMCHUAM)

3 cups (750 g) sugar
1 cup (250 mL) water
15–20 jasmine flowers and few drops jasmine essence, or 15–20 rose petals and 1 teaspoon rosewater
3–4 large oranges or mandarins (tangerines) divided into segments, with pith removed

In a large saucepan, combine sugar and water. Bring to the boil, then simmer for 10 minutes until sugar dissolves and a syrup forms. If necessary, strain syrup through cheesecloth. Cool, then add either jasmine essence or rosewater.

Place orange or mandarin segments in a large serving bowl and pour the syrup over them. Garnish with jasmine or rose petals and serve immediately.

Serves 4

BANANAS IN COCONUT SAUCE
(GLUAY BUAT CHEE)

6 large bananas, peeled
1½ cups (375 mL) coconut milk
1½ tablespoons sugar
pinch salt

Slice bananas diagonally into 2 cm slices. Heat coconut milk in a saucepan, then add sugar and salt. Bring to the boil and simmer, stirring, for 2 minutes.

Remove from heat and stir in banana slices. Return to the boil for 10 seconds. Remove from heat and serve with ice cream or sticky rice (see recipe).

Serves 4–6

Steamed Whole Pumpkin with Coconut Custard chilled and cut into wedges.

STEAMED WHOLE PUMPKIN WITH COCONUT CUSTARD
(SANGKAYA FAK TONG)

1.5 kg pumpkin, with good colour and shape (see Note)
8 eggs, beaten
1 cup (250 mL) thick coconut milk
½ cup (125 g) sugar, castor or brown

Neatly cut off the pumpkin top with stem and retain for a lid. Try not to make the opening too big. Scoop out pulp and seeds, leaving a thick layer of pumpkin meat. Rinse out well and pat dry thoroughly.

In a large mixing bowl, beat together eggs, coconut milk and sugar, pour into the pumpkin and cover with its 'lid'.

Gently place pumpkin in a large steamer and cook for 30–45 minutes until custard is firm and pumpkin tender. Test with a skewer. Cool, remove and chill overnight. Cut into thick wedges and serve.

Note: If using a large, tough pumpkin you may have to steam it upside down in a steamer for 10 minutes first, cool, pat dry, then fill with custard and steam again another 30 minutes or so.

Serves 6

COCONUT ICE CREAM
(ICE CREAM KATI)

1¼ cups (300 mL) thick coconut milk
1½ cups (375 mL) fresh cream
4 eggs, with 2 yolks separated
1 teaspoon vanilla or rosewater (optional)
½ cup (125 g) sugar
½ teaspoon salt
50 g shredded coconut (sweetened), dry-fried until golden
fresh mint sprigs

In a saucepan, heat coconut milk and cream over medium heat, so they cook for several minutes without boiling. In a bowl, beat together 2 eggs and 2 extra yolks, vanilla, sugar and salt. Pour into a double-boiler over boiling water, and gradually beat in warm coconut milk mixture, a few tablespoons at a time. Stir until the mixture thickens to coat the back of a spoon. Remove from heat and cool, stirring occasionally.

Pour into a metal ice cream tray and put in the coldest part of the freezer until half frozen, about 1 hour. Scoop into a food processor or chilled bowl and beat thoroughly until smooth. Pour into metal tray again and freeze completely. Serve in scoops, garnished with shredded coconut and mint sprigs.

Serves 4

1. Prepare pumpkin by scooping out pulp and seeds. Rinse well and pat dry.

2. Pour custard mix into pumpkin and cover with pumpkin lid.

3. Steam pumpkin for 30–45 minutes. Test with a skewer.

1. Strain custard through muslin or cheese-cloth so the mixture is fine and smooth.

2. Steam until firm.

BANANA PANCAKES
(KANOM GLUAY HOM)

500 g ripe bananas, mashed
½ cup (60 g) flour
½ cup (125 g) white sugar
1 cup (250 mL) thick coconut cream or canned coconut milk
3 tablespoons dried coconut, sweetened or unsweetened (see Note)
2 teaspoons vegetable oil

In a large mixing bowl, add small quantities of mashed banana, flour, sugar, coconut cream and dried coconut (reserving a little for garnishing). Beat well with a fork or mixer and continue to add remaining ingredients until you have a pancake batter that's fairly thick.

Heat an oiled frypan over moderate heat and, when hot, pour in enough batter to make a pancake about 7.5 cm in diameter. When pancake bubbles on surface, flip over and cook until golden on the other side. Repeat for the rest. Serve with ice cream or Coconut Custard (see recipe) and garnish with dried coconut.

Serves 4

Coconut Custard steamed and served garnished in individual bowls. You may eat the jasmine if you're feeling adventurous. Don't eat the banana leaf triangles.

COCONUT CUSTARD
(SANGKAYA)

1 cup (250 mL) thick coconut milk
4 eggs, beaten
½ cup (125 g) sugar

Beat coconut milk, eggs and sugar together until sugar dissolves and mixture is well blended. Sieve through muslin or cheesecloth so the mixture is fine and smooth, place in a serving bowl inside a steamer and steam until firm. Alternatively, you can steam the custard in individual serving bowls.

Serves 4

Note: For dried coconut, buy dried coconut flesh at Asian or health food stores. If unavailable, use ordinary unsweetened desiccated coconut.

CUSTARD SQUARES
(KANOM MO KAENG)

In Thailand this popular dessert is usually steamed but this recipe is adapted for oven baking.

2 cups (500 mL) thick coconut milk
7 eggs, beaten
½ cup (125 g) sugar, preferably brown
1 tablespoon rosewater (optional)
2 tablespoons desiccated or shredded coconut

Preheat oven to 180°C (350°F) and grease a shallow rectangular or square baking dish (about 15 cm square). Beat together all ingredients in a large bowl.

In a double boiler or a large bowl set on top of a steamer, stir the mixture over boiling water until it thickens to the consistency of soft scrambled eggs. Pour into the baking dish and bake for 30 minutes.

Remove and place under a griller on medium heat. Grill until the top of the custard is golden. It takes only a few minutes so be careful it doesn't burn. Remove, cool and chill, then cut into 4 cm squares.

Serves 4–6

TROPICAL FRUITS IN JASMINE OR LIME SYRUP
(PONLAMAI NAMCHUAM)

This simple syrup with a combination of tropical fruits of your choice can make a stunning dessert, especially if served in a hollowed, decorated watermelon or other smooth-skinned melon. If you don't have the time, simply serve in an attractive glass bowl.

2 cups (500 mL) water
500 g sugar
few drops jasmine essence or lime or lemon zest
1 small rock melon, scooped into balls
1 small honeydew melon, scooped into balls
1 small pawpaw, scooped into balls
1 small pineapple, diced
assorted cherries, lychees, seedless grapes or other favourite fruit
fresh mint leaves, to garnish

Tropical Fruits in Jasmine Syrup. If you don't have an elaborately carved watermelon on hand, use a large clear glass bowl.

In a saucepan bring water, sugar and jasmine essence to the boil. Cook for 10 minutes until it forms a syrup. Taste to see whether extra jasmine essence is required. If the syrup is not completely clear, cool and strain through cheesecloth.

Arrange fruits in serving bowl and pour enough syrup over to cover them. Chill and serve. Alternatively, pour syrup over the fruit, chill, then spoon into a hollowed, chilled melon. Garnish with mint leaves.

Serves 6–8

MAKE YOUR OWN COCONUT MILK
For the best tasting coconut milk prepare your own by soaking 150 g desiccated coconut in 1½ cups (375 mL) hot water for 5 minutes; blend in a blender, strain through muslin or cotton cloth and squeeze out rich milk.

THREE THAI BANQUETS

A typical Thai meal consists of rice and at least five other dishes. There's usually a soup, a fried dish, a curry, something steamed or braised, and a salad of cooked or raw vegetables. Dessert is often a simple platter of assorted fresh fruit.

If you want to have a traditional Thai dinner, you can sit on the floor, serve everything at once and eat with forks and spoons. Today, however, most urban Thai families eat Western style. If you really want to get serious about traditional Thai, you should try

to have a few hot sauces on hand. The Thais serve at least one and sometimes several at a meal. They're a bit like the spicy, hot sambals of Java and Bali. Some varieties are commercially available, but the best are homemade.

2. THAI BANQUET (TRADITIONAL) for 8–10 people

Savoury Seafood Rolls (Hae Guen)
Sweet Pork (Muu Wan) snack sized pieces
Hot and Sour Chilli Sauce (Nam Prik Keega)
Sweet and Sour Cucumber Relish (Thang Kwa Preow Wan)
Stir-fried Ginger Chicken (Pad King Gai)
Salted Fish (Pla Kem)
Chilli Prawns (Goong Pad Prik)
Muslim Beef Curry (Gaeng Mussaman Nua)
Flaked Fish and Tamarind Sauce (Nam Prik Tha Dang)
Steamed Rice (Khao Plow)
Stuffed Cucumber Soup (Gaeng Chud Thang Kwa Sod Sai)
Great Salad (Yam Yai)
Duck Casserole (Tom Kem Ped)
Assorted Fresh Fruit (Ponlamai)

1. THAI BANQUET (WESTERN STYLE) for 8–10 people

Mixed Satays (Satay)
Satay Sauce (Nam Jim Satay)
Thai Spring Rolls (Poh Pia)
Sweet and Sour Cucumber Relish (Thang Kwa Preow Wan)
Sweet Chilli Dipping Sauce (Nam Jim Wan)
Spicy Prawn Soup (Tom Yam Goong)
Steamed Rice (Khao Plow)
Green Sweet Chicken Curry (Gaeng Keow Wan Gai)
Whole Fish in Red Curry Sauce with Lime Leaves (Gaeng Pla Choo Chee)
Stir-fried Mixed Vegetables (Pad Pak Ruam)
Sweet and Sour Crisp Fried Thai Noodles (Mee Grob)
Prawn Salad with Lemon Grass and Mint (Yam Pla Goong)
Marinated Braised Beef with Cucumber (Nua Ob)
Pork Salad with Mint, Peanuts and Ginger (Nam Sod)
Mangoes with Sticky Rice (Mamuang Khao Nieo)

3. SEAFOOD BANQUET for 6–8 people

Spicy Deep-fried Fish Cakes (Tod Man Pla)
Sweet and Sour Cucumber Relish (Thang Kwa Preow Wan)
Prawn and Pork Toast (Kanom Pang Muu Goong)
Spicy Prawn Soup (Tom Yam Goong)
Stir-fried Seafood with Fresh Herbs (Ahahn Talay)
Whole Fish with Ginger Sauce (Pla Jian)
Spicy Mussels with Chilli and Lime Leaves (Gaeng Choo Chee Hoi Mang Pu)
Prawn Salad with Lemon Grass and Mint (Yam Pla Goong)
Great Salad (Yam Yai)
Steamed Rice (Khao Plow)
Banana Pancakes (Kanom Gluay Hom)

SOME IDEAS FOR MENUS

In this chapter, we've selected a range of meals but you'll have to adjust the recipes occasionally to suit the number of diners. Most recipes have 200–300 g of the main ingredient (e.g. meat, seafood, vegetable) so you can expect four to six people to get a reasonable taste of each dish. Most of the meals are intended to be shared by four people, but each meal is generally equivalent to one main course.

Read every recipe carefully and make your own judgement about how hungry your guests are likely to be, then plan and adjust accordingly. We've included some Western-style Thai banquets, some traditional ones and some ideas for menus for varying numbers of people.

4. THAI STYLE DINNER for 6–8 people

Spicy Deep-fried Fish Cakes (Tod Man Pla)
Sweet and Sour Cucumber Relish (Thang Kwa Preow Wan)
Crisp Deep-fried Vegetables (Pak Tod)
Sweet Chilli Dipping Sauce (Nam Jim Wan)
Spicy Chicken, Coconut and Galangal Soup (Tom Kah Gai)
Red Pork Curry (Gaeng Ped Muu)
Beef with Basil, Chilli and Green Beans (Nua Pad Krapao)
Prawns with Garlic and Pepper served with Greens (Goong Tod Grateum)
Calamari Salad with Mint, Onion and Lemon Grass (Yam Pla Meuk)
Carrot and Green Bean Salad with Pawpaw (Som Tam)
Steamed Rice (Khao Plow)
Bananas in Coconut Sauce (Gluay Buat Chee)

5. THAI STYLE DINNER for 6–8 people

Prawn Satay (Goong Satay)
Satay Sauce (Nam Jim Satay)
Crispy Parcels (Keio Grob)
Sweet and Sour Cucumber Relish (Thang Kwa Preow Wan)
Sweet Chilli Dipping Sauce (Nam Jim Wan)
Pumpkin and Coconut Cream Soup (Gaeng Liang Fak Tong)
Sweet and Sour Pork Spare Ribs (Preow Wan Graduk Muu)
Whole Fish with Ginger Sauce (Pla Jian)
Steamed Spicy Chicken (Haw Mok Gai)
Rose Petal and Watercress Salad (Yam Dok Gulab)
Steamed Rice (Khao Plow)
Oranges in Rose or Jasmine Syrup (Som Namchuam)
Assorted Fresh Fruit (Ponlamai)

6. TRADITIONAL THAI DINNER for 6–8 people

Barbecued Pork with Somi's Spicy Jittra Dipping Sauce (Jittra Muu Yahng)
Duck Steamed with Chinese Melon and Pickled Limes (Ped Thoon Manao Dong)
Chiang Mai Noodles (Khao Soi Chiang Mai)
Salted Fish (Pla Kem)
Assorted Raw Vegetable Pieces with Spicy Dried Shrimp Sauce (Nam Prik Kapi)
Spicy Beef Curry (Gaeng Pa Nua)
Chilli Fish Sauce (Nam Pla Prik)
Steamed Rice (Khao Plow)
Assorted Fresh Fruit (Ponlamai)

7. SEAFOOD DINNER for 4–6 people

Spicy Deep-fried Fish Cakes (Tod Man Pla)
Sweet and Sour Cucumber Relish (Thang Kwa Preow Wan)
Vegetable and Prawn Soup (Gaeng Liang)
Spicy Mussels with Chilli and Lime Leaves (Gaeng Choo Chee Hoi Mang Pu)
Whole Fish with Fresh Chilli, Garlic and Coriander (Pla Lad Prik)
Prawn Salad with Lemon Grass and Mint (Yam Pla Goong)
Green Mango Salad (Yam Mamuang)
Steamed Rice (Khao Plow)
Steamed Whole Pumpkin with Coconut Custard (Sangkaya Fak Tong)

8. EASY THAI DINNER for 4–6 people

Steamed Mussels with Lime Leaves and Galangal (Hoi Mang Pu Ob Mordin)
Spicy Chicken, Coconut and Galangal Soup (Tom Kah Gai)
Chilli Beef (Nua Pad Prik)
Prawns with Garlic and Pepper served with Greens (Goong Tod Grateum)
Red Pork Curry (Gaeng Ped Muu)
Steamed Rice (Khao Plow)
Assorted Fresh Fruit (Ponlamai)

9. MILDLY SPICED THAI MEAL for 4–6 people

Crisp Fried Calamari (Pla Meuk Tod)
Sweet Chilli Dipping Sauce (Nam Jim Wan)
Garlic Lamb (Nua Gae Tod Grateum)
Vegetable and Prawn Soup (Gaeng Liang)
Chicken Salad with Mint, Onion and Lemon Grass (Laab Gai)
Mixed Vegetables in Coconut Sauce (Pak Tom Kati)
Simple Fried Rice (Khao Pad Tamada)
Thai Fried Bananas (Gluay Tod)

INGREDIENTS

ASIAN BROCCOLI, CHINESE CABBAGE

These are two of the now extensive range of Asian green vegetables available in Chinatowns and larger Asian grocery stores outside Asia. Even larger fruit markets now offer a range of Asian vegetables. European broccoli and cabbage can be substituted but it is worth trying the Asian varieties.

BASIL (BAI HORAPA)

There are three types of fresh basil leaves used in Thai cooking. European sweet basil will substitute for all of them. Look for the Thai varieties in Chinatowns in larger cities. Bai Horapa is the nearest to European sweet basil and is readily found in Asian shops. Bai Manglak has tiny leaves like dwarf basil and the Thais sprinkle it over salads and soups. Bai Krapao has the strongest flavour. Its leaves are a reddish purple and are used cooked. Basil is available at larger fruit markets and is easy to grow at home.

CHILLI (PRIK)

Not all Thai dishes are hot, but chillies are synonymous with Thai cuisine. So much so, it's hard to believe they were only introduced to Thailand after being discovered by Christopher Columbus' expedition to the New World less than 500 years ago. Fresh chillies come in red, green and yellow and in various sizes. Usually the smaller they are, the hotter they taste. Dried chillies are widely available and if necessary can be soaked in hot water for a few minutes before using. Ground chillies, chilli paste or dried chilli flakes can be substituted in some dishes.

To lessen the hotness, use larger chillies and remove the seeds. If you're not used to hot food you can often delete the chilli altogether, and when called for in garnishing, use capsicum strips instead. The taste grows on you, however, and you'll be surprised how quickly your tolerance for chilli improves. A warning — take great care when slicing and preparing chillies. Wash your hands and nails thoroughly after handling them, and keep your hands away from your face and eyes, and from those of children. The oils the chilli skins exude are volatile.

CHILLI PASTE (NAM PRIK PAO) (sometimes called Chilli Paste in Bean Oil, Burnt Mild or Roasted Chilli Paste)

This is an ingredient in many Thai recipes, including the famous Tom Yam soups. The paste is made in Thailand and sold in squat jars in the condiments or Thai sections of Asian foodstores. Made from dried chillies, dried shrimp, roasted onion and garlic, sugar and tamarind juice; a small amount of fresh or dried chilli can be used as a substitute.

CHILLI SAUCE (NAM PRIK)

There are countless recipes for chilli sauces, to bottle as condiments and to make fresh to accompany noodles and rice, the way Italian sauces accompany spaghetti. Some of the famous Thai bottled sauces, Saus Prik, include 'Sriracha' and 'Sweet Chilli Sauce for Chicken' (it goes with everything, in fact). There are many recipes for homemade traditional spicy hot sauces — no traditional Thai meal would be complete without at least one.

CHINESE FIVE SPICE

A brown powdered mixture of star anise, cloves, cinnamon, pepper and fennel, it is used in roast meat and poultry dishes, and is sold in packets or jars in Asian foodstores.

CHINESE GREEN MELON (FAK-KEOW) (sometimes called bitter melon, balsam pear, kareala or bitter gourd)

This is an elongated, wrinkled green fruit sold fresh in Chinatowns; it can also be bought canned in Asian foodstores. Chokos or cucumbers can be substituted.

COCONUT (MAPRAO) AND COCONUT MILK (NAM KATI)

Flaked or shredded coconut meat and desiccated coconut are rarely used except for sweets and garnishes. But coconut milk (pulped flesh, not juice) is one of the most important ingredients. It's used in curries, meat, vegetable and seafood dishes as well as for desserts and sweets. You can make your own by placing 100 g desiccated (dried) coconut with 300 mL hot water in a saucepan and simmering over a low heat for about 5 minutes. Strain through a sieve, pushing down on the pulp with the back of a spoon. This will yield roughly 1 cup (250 mL) of thick coconut milk. A second pressing will give you a thinner milk; just repeat the process using the used coconut and a little less water.

Alternatively, put the warm water and the coconut in a blender, blend for 1—2 minutes and sieve. Coconut cream can be skimmed from the top of the milk after it has stood for a few hours in the refrigerator. The easy way out (and sometimes the cheapest) is to buy ready-made, canned coconut milk at major supermarkets. Instant coconut milk powder is now available and is a handy substitute.

CORIANDER (PAK CHEE) (sometimes called Chinese Parsley or Cilantro)

Fresh coriander is essential to Thai cuisine. The leaves flavour stir-fried dishes, sauces and curries, and garnish practically everything. The roots and stems are either chopped finely or pounded for marinades and curry pastes. Coriander is now easy to get in larger fruit markets and Asian grocery stores or you can easily grow your own. You can freeze the roots and the first few centimetres of the stems, wrapped in plastic. When thawed, they're a bit soggy, but they retain their flavour and they really are indispensible. Coriander seeds are sometimes used in curry pastes, too. There really is no substitute for the flavour of fresh coriander, but when called for only as a garnish, you can use any fresh herb leaves.

DRIED KAFFIR LIME LEAVES (MAKRUT)

The Kaffir lime is a little-known member of the citrus family. The fruit has a dark warty green rind and little juice, but the skin is rich in aromatic oils. The Thais use the lime zest and the leaves (Bai Makrut). Fresh leaves are hard to find outside Asia, but ordinary lime zest and young citrus leaves make reasonable substitutes. However, dried Kaffir lime leaves are available at most Asian foodstores and are inexpensive. You do not have to soak them if they are to go into casseroles or any dish which has enough liquid and cooks them longer than a few minutes, which is necessary to revitalise them. But if you want to slice them into shreds (and this is specified sometimes in our recipes) then you will need to soak them, preferably in warm water for 5—10 minutes to cut them.

EGGPLANTS/AUBERGINES (MAKEUA PUONG)

There are many sizes and varieties of eggplant grown in Thailand. They come in white, green, yellow and purple, and taste similar to European kinds. The smallest Thai eggplant is the pea eggplant (makeua puong) which can sometimes be found in Asian foodstores. These little eggplants are used in curries, but as you may have difficulty finding this ingredient, we have substituted green peas.

FISH SAUCE (NAM PLA)

Fish sauce is to the Thais what soy sauce is to the Chinese and Japanese. It's a watery, amber-coloured, clear sauce, made from salted and fermented fish. Nam means water and pla means fish. It's rich in protein and B vitamins and its use is widespread. Fish sauce is available in supermarkets and Asian foodstores, is inexpensive and lasts, unrefrigerated, indefinitely. Thai or Chinese brands are acceptable.

GALANGAL (KAH) (also called Laos in Indonesia, galangale [Old English], or Siamese Ginger)

A member of the ginger family, galangal is a pale yellow root with pink knobs and sprouts. It's sold as dried pieces in Asian foodstores, or powdered, in health stores. One teaspoon of powder equals roughly a 0.5 cm slice. If you need to slice dried galangal pieces, soak them in hot water for at least 10 minutes. Thais believe galangal has medicinal digestive qualities as well as being a fragrant spice. Our fresh green ginger root is not a substitute.

GARLIC (GRATEUM)

Thai garlic is smaller and more tender than ours and is not peeled before use. Pickled garlic is a common snack and ingredient in many noodle dishes and in Thailand is pickled in whole knobs. European garlic should be peeled unless it's very young and tender. Chopped fried garlic (grateum jeow) can be purchased in stores and is delicious in Thai soups and noodle dishes.

HOISIN SAUCE

A sweet, spicy, reddish brown sauce from Chinese cuisine, it is made from soy beans and is usually sold in cans or bottles. Used to marinate roast meats or poultry in Chinese cooking, it can also be combined with other sauces as a dip and is an ingredient in some Thai dishes.

LEMON GRASS (TAKRAI)

This favourite Thai herb grows in clumps of tall, slim green reeds, and looks a bit like a large freesia without flowers. Use the pale lower part of the stalk which can be chopped finely, or bruise the tougher, greener part of the stem with a pestle, if larger pieces are called for.

Lemon grass is easy to grow or you can buy it in bunches at Asian vegetable markets.

You can also buy dried lemon grass at Asian grocers, or powdered at health food stores. Fresh is far superior. In an emergency, substitute dried (soaked for ½ hour) or 3 or 4 strips of lemon peel for 1 tablespoon of lemon grass.

LESSER GINGER (KRACHAI)

This is available dried in packets at Asian foodstores. It is sold under the English name of Powdered Rhizome when used as a powder, or simply as Rhizome when it takes the form of dried, slivered roots. It has a mild flavour and recipes will not suffer too much if you delete it.

LIMES (MANAO)

Not to be confused with Kaffir limes, the Thais use small dark green limes for their juice and to garnish salads. If you don't have limes on hand, substitute lemons for juice and lemon wedges for garnishes. When you see limes or lemons at bargain prices, buy and freeze them. They're often called for in Thai cooking and though they're a bit mushy when defrosted, their juice is quite acceptable. They can be thawed in seconds in the microwave. Alternatively, juice them and freeze the juice in ice cube containers.

Pickled limes, or pickled lemons as they're sometimes labelled, you can buy at Asian stores. Included in this book is a recipe for pickled lemons, the only drawback being that you have to keep them for 3 months before you can use them.

MUSHROOMS (HED, HED HOM)

Thais use two types of mushrooms. Dried Chinese mushrooms (called Hed Hom) are used in clear soups and some stir-fried dishes. They need to be soaked in warm water for 20 minutes and their stems discarded. Dried Chinese mushrooms are easy to find at Asian stores.

Thai straw mushrooms can be bought in cans or jars at Asian stores. You can substitute canned champignons or fresh button mushrooms if necessary.

NOODLES (MEE)

Here are the four most common noodles used in Thailand:

Cellophane Noodles (Woon Sen)

Made from mung bean flour, they're also called bean-thread noodles, bean vermicelli or glass noodles. They're used in soups and some stir-fried dishes and are tough and semi-transparent before cooking. Always soak for several minutes in water before using.

Rice Vermicelli (Sen Mee)

Made from rice, they're also called rice sticks or rice noodles. They vary in size from narrow vermicelli to wider, ribbon-shaped noodles about 0.5 cm wide. The larger noodles should be soaked for at least ½ hour in warm water, the thinner noodles 10 minutes. It's important to drain them well before using. The only time you don't need to soak them is for Sweet and Sour Crisp Fried Thai Noodles. Then they puff up when fried in hot oil.

Egg Noodles (Ba Mee)

Egg and wheat-flour noodles come from China and Thailand. They're nice on their own with a spicy Thai sauce, especially with any of the dipping sauces. They're also used in stir-fry dishes and soups. Available in large supermarkets and Asian stores.

Fresh Rice Noodles (Gwaytio)

Packaged wet and folded into a block, you'll often see them on the counter at Asian foodstores in Chinatown, or in the refrigerated section. Unwrap but don't unravel them. Simply slice them while folded into whatever size you want. Use in soups or stir-fried dishes.

OYSTER SAUCE (NAMMAN HOI)

A Chinese sauce made from oysters. It's thick, brown, rich and salty and should be used sparingly. Oyster sauce is readily available at most supermarkets now, and in Asian stores.

PICKLED SOY BEAN (TAO CHEOW) (sometimes called fermented or salted soy beans)

This is sold in bottles in Asian foodstores, with a label in English which says Yellow Bean Sauce. Not an essential ingredient, it can be deleted from a recipe without affecting the flavour too much.

PICKLED WHITE RADISH

These are dried and salted Chinese white radishes usually found in plastic bags in Asian foodstores. They keep indefinitely; simply slice a few pieces off when you need some.

RICE (KHAO) (Long-grain and Sticky Rice)

The Thais use two main varieties — long-grain polished rice, and sticky or glutinous rice. Long-grain is served with all meals, and is usually steamed or cooked in rice-cookers so it's light and fluffy. The absorption method also works well. Rinse the rice, then place in a saucepan (which has a lid) and cover the top of the rice with about 3 cm (or one knuckle's length) of water. Boil rapidly until the water is level with the rice and tunnels appear on the surface. Cover with a tight-fitting lid and turn the heat to very low or off. The rice should be cooked after about 10 minutes. Do not remove the lid (apart from a quick check) until you're ready to serve. Before serving, fluff up with a fork or chopstick.

Sticky or glutinous rice can be bought at Asian foodstores and takes the place of ordinary rice in the north and north-eastern regions of Thailand, where it is the mainstay of traditional diets (although these days plain long and short-grain rice are making inroads in the region). In central Thailand, sticky rice is used mainly in sweets, particularly for the Thai favourite, Mangoes with Sticky Rice. The secret is to rinse the rice several times and soak it for at least 2 hours, then cook it in a steamer.

SALT
Most day-to-day meals, stir-fried dishes and salads do not use salt at all. In the traditional cuisine, salt is rarely used as a flavouring, but as a preservative. You may find salt where fish sauce isn't used — in curry pastes and spicy sauces, pickling recipes such as pickled garlic, salted meats and fish where it's used to aid preserving, and in some desserts (but this use of salt is to satisfy Western palates). Many Thais don't bother with salt. Their plain rice and noodles, for example, are not salted.

SESAME OIL
This oil, extracted from sesame seeds, has a very strong, nutty flavour. It is most often used in Chinese cooking as a flavouring in soups and stir-fried dishes. It is sold in bottles in Asian foodstores and sometimes at larger supermarkets.

SHRIMP, DRIED (DRIED SHRIMP), DRIED PRAWNS (KUNG HENG)
Small salted prawns, dried in the sun, that are sold in packets in Asian foodstores and need to be soaked in warm water for about 20 minutes before using. Dry, they're often pounded and added to pastes and salads or used as a garnish for noodle dishes. Thai and Chinese brands are available.

SHRIMP PASTE, PRAWN PASTE (KAPI) (also called by the Malay name, Blanchan)
It's hard to believe that such a strong-smelling pungent paste can enhance the flavour of anything, but this is a vital ingredient in Thai cuisine. It ranges from a syrupy, pink sauce to a hard, brown, compacted slab. It's made from dried prawns and salt, is rich in B vitamins and, together with fish sauce, is an important source of protein in South-east Asian diets. The fresh paste available in jars needs refrigeration. The thick dried pastes do not. But they do need airtight containers because their fishy odour is overwhelming. This paste must be stir-fried or roasted in foil before you can eat it. Anchovy paste can be substituted, but shrimp paste is easy to find at Asian stores.

STAR ANISE
Star-shaped seed cluster containing shiny brown seeds. Not related to the well-known anise seed, but to the magnolia family. Used extensively in Chinese cooking, it is readily available.

TAMARIND (MAK KAM PIAK)
Tamarind adds an interesting sour or sharp taste to Thai curries and fish dishes in particular, without the tartness of lemons. The tamarind tree is native to Asia and has fern-like leaves and pods with doughy flesh. When ripe, the pod is brown and brittle on the outside but the pulp is juicy. You can buy tamarind pulp in packets at Asian stores and in health stores. You can also buy jars of either tamarind concentrate (strained pulp) or tamarind liquid. The pulp needs to be soaked in warm water and strained to get tamarind juice. The longer it soaks, the stronger the juice. The concentrate requires the addition of water: 1 teaspoon of tamarind needs roughly 2 tablespoons of water, but this varies, so check the label. Lemon, lime or orange juice can be substitutes; so can a mixture of 6 parts vinegar and 1 part sugar.

TURMERIC (KAMIN)
Its use in Thai cuisine reflects the Indian influence. Thais use turmeric in curries and sometimes to colour rice. Though it can be bought fresh in Thailand, it's hard to find fresh elsewhere. However, you can buy it powdered in supermarkets everywhere. Turmeric is a relative of the ginger and arrowroot families and is a bright yellowish orange. Traditionally it was used to colour the robes of Thai monks.

WOOD FUNGUS, WOOD MUSHROOMS (HED HUNU)
Not an essential ingredient by any means, but its use in several Thai dishes reflects the Chinese influence. You can buy wood fungus at Asian stores and it keeps indefinitely. It looks like dried bits of burnt paper but when soaked in water turns into a jelly-like brown substance and is a component of some stir-fried dishes. Always soak before using.

Glossary of Terms

AUSTRALIA	UK	USA
Equipment and terms		
can	tin	can
crushed	minced	pressed
frying pan	frying pan	skillet
grill	grill	broil
paper towel	kitchen paper	white paper towel
plastic wrap	cling film	plastic wrap
seeded	stoned	pitted
Ingredients		
beetroot	beetroot	beets
capsicum	pepper	sweep pepper
caster sugar	caster sugar	granulated table sugar
cornflour	cornflour	cornstarch
cream	single cream	light or coffee cream
desiccated coconut	desiccated coconut	shredded coconut
eggplant	aubergine	eggplant
five spice	Chinese spice combination of cinnamon, cloves, fennel, star anise and Szechuan pepper	
flour	plain flour	all-purpose flour
green cabbage	white or roundhead cabbage	cabbage
pawpaw	pawpaw	papaya or papaw
prawn	prawn or shrimp	shrimp
shallot	spring onion	scallion
snow pea	mangetout, sugar pea	snow pea
thickened cream	double cream	heavy or whipping cream
tomato puree	tomato puree	tomato paste
tomato sauce	tomato sauce	tomato ketchup
yoghurt	natural yoghurt	unflavoured yoghurt
zucchini	courgette	zucchini

Oven Temperatures

	Celsius	Fahrenheit
Very slow	120	250
Slow	140–150	275–300
Moderately slow	160	325
Moderate	180	350
Moderately hot	190	375
Hot	200	400
	220	425
	230	450
Very hot	250–260	475–500

INDEX